The Logbooks

A DRIFTLESS CONNECTICUT SERIES BOOK

This book is a 2014 selection in the Driftless Connecticut Series, for an outstanding book in any field on a Connecticut topic or written by a Connecticut author.

ALSO BY ANNE FARROW

Complicity: How the North Promoted,
Prolonged, and Profited from Slavery

(2005; with Joel Lang & Jenifer Frank)

WESLEYAN UNIVERSITY PRESS
MIDDLETOWN, CONNECTICUT

ANNE FARROW

The Logbooks

CONNECTICUT'S SLAVE SHIPS
AND HUMAN MEMORY

Wesleyan University Press

Middletown CT 06459

www.wesleyan.edu/wespress

© 2014 Anne Farrow

All rights reserved

Manufactured in the United States of America

Designed by Eric M. Brooks

Typeset in Monotype Bell by Passumpsic Publishing

*The Driftless Connecticut Series is funded by the
Beatrice Fox Auerbach Foundation Fund
at the Hartford Foundation for Public Giving.*

Library of Congress Cataloging-in-Publication Data
available upon request

5 4 3 2 1

FOR STEPHEN,

who has a verdant heart

...le Imploy'd abo rigging Carp. & Joiner making awning
...r Making a Pump Can ⸺ No Trade at all ⸺

...rday July 15th 1758 this 24 hours Light Winds & pleas. We
...e Imploy'd overhawling Blocks Carpr. & Joiner Making
...ng ⸺ No Trade only Bought some Corn & plantins

...ay July 16th. this 24 hours Light Winds & pleas. Wea. People
...yd abo. Jobs Carp. & Joiner abo. the awning the Cap. on
...d Wanton No Tea Purchased one boy Slave of Quaquome

...day July 17. this 24 hours Light Winds & pleas. Wea. Geop
...loyd over hawling tobacco Carp. & Joiner abo. the awning
...ade at all ⸺ Saild for Sirrenam the Large Dutch Sh
...500 & od Slaves onboard

...ay July 18. this 24 hours Light Winds & pleas. Wea. People
...y in y. Hold & fetching Brazeal Tobacco from a Dutch
...Cap. Buley ⸺ Purchased one man Slave ⸺

...esday July 19. this 24 hours Light Winds but a Large S
...le Imploy'd picking Tobacco No Trade at all ⸺

...day July 20. this 24 hours Calm & little Wind People Imploy
...Hold Cooper a Cutting Rum Hd Purchased old Two Slave
...essels in y. Rhode except Three Poor Rum Men
...d the yaul up to Clean ⸺ braught a bl Beef

...y July 20 this 24 hours Calm Weather People Imployd over
...ld & found a Hogs. No 86 Leaked all out No 85 only 54 Gal. in b
...gin to y. Cap. ⸺ Leakage ocationed by all y. Head Hoops fly
...rade this 24 hours the agr'd with my Lord to send a man
...to accraw after y. Longboat for 4 Gal. Trade Rum ⸺

...urday July 21 this 24 hours Calm Wea. People Imployd fill
...heads with Water & with Rum Cooper a Cutting Hogs
...d from y. Longboat by a Letter from Underwood w
...g at Mumford with 3 Slaves on board

...day July 22. this 24 hours Calm & hazey Weather at 10
...ye Ship to W. Ward which we Suppos'd to be the English Man of

Contents

Color photographs follow page 96

Preface

"Why are you doing this?" my friend asked.

I looked at her lean brown face, lit by the glass lamps suspended over our restaurant table, and made what I did not recognize, then, as an excuse.

"New England's relationship with slavery is a great story," I said. "We're journalists; we're supposed to uncover stories of wrong and injustice." I made my argument, or, as we called it in the newsroom, my pitch.

Liz looked at me for a long moment with the level, answering gaze I knew from having had her edit my stories at the newspaper.

"That's not it," she said. "When white people take up black stuff, there's always a reason. There's always *something* there."

I told her that I needed engaging work, having recently broken up with my longtime boyfriend. Studying my country's tortured relationship with slavery and race prejudice made my own life, with its varied griefs and money worries, seem small.

She smiled at me as if to say, *that's not it,* and picked up her menu.

Truthfully, I had not thought about why I was researching the history of slavery in America until my friend asked me. The work had begun as an assignment for the Sunday magazine of the newspaper where I worked, and then deepened into a book coauthored with two colleagues. But always, I worked at the direction of others.

Three years into the work and engaged by it without ever knowing why, I found the raw material of New England slaveholding so gripping that I didn't pause to ask. The stories of the captives pulled me forward and then cracked my heart, and they were everywhere—in newspapers, court records, diaries, and census lists. A six-year-old girl with an African name whose owners were questioned after she died of a beating. An advertisement for a runaway black man who fled with a coarse brown coat and his violin. A man who wanted to sell his slave because she would not stop weeping.

I wanted to protect them, but could do nothing for them except continue my research, and write about what I was finding.

I began to read about memory, and learned that Sigmund Freud believed the unconscious self never lies. That it *cannot* lie. And then I saw my parents. My father, a civil rights lawyer, had died several years earlier, at eighty-seven, and my mother had been diagnosed with dementia six months after his death. Neat in the London Fog raincoat he had bought her, she held my hand in a Stop and Shop parking lot the week after his death and asked, softly, "Am I alive?" I looked at her and felt an absolute responsibility settle onto me. I caressed her arm and thought, but did not say, *you will forget me.*

From that October day, she lived seven years, dying just a few days after the anniversary of Dad's death.

I expected her to become helpless, and she did. What I did not expect was that by the time she died in my arms on a rainy fall afternoon, she would teach me about the workings of human memory. In watching her memory fade and then unravel, I learned that there is a core of memories that remains yet is altered profoundly by time and the progression of the disease.

I couldn't avoid the contrast between what was happening to my mother's memory and the historical memory I was studying, which seemed so fractured and incomplete.

New England's memories of its relationship with enslavement had the quality of fortified recollection. Yes, there were slaves, I read, but they were treated more as family members. There were slaves in New England, but not that many. Slavery was not profitable for New Englanders because we didn't grow cotton. New England had very little to do with American slavery except ending it.

These were the assumptions most frequently expressed to me, even though numerous historians over the past half century have explored the killing realities of New England enslavement. Despite the work of these scholars, the benign and cherished myths are still held close. The popular narrative hasn't changed. Henry Louis Gates Jr. says that America has a kind of "amnesia" around the story of American enslavement. We've forgotten our history, then forgotten that we forgot it. Slavery is not the book that we know we own but can't find; we don't even know it's on our shelves. This is a book tucked behind other books, and we can't see it.

We will always want to present ourselves in the best light, to say that a black man wasn't hired because no black men applied, or to maintain that Northerners didn't have slaves because we didn't grow cotton. We want to do right, but it's hard, and we may not succeed. Why not stick with the story we already have? The one that's already in the books?

Yet we are responsible to the truth as it was lived in earlier centuries.

Dori Laub, the great scholar of Holocaust remembrance, says that we have to know our buried truths in order to live our lives. None of us is free if we keep silent.

I believe that Americans still do not have a shared and meaningful body of knowledge about a labor system here that held millions in bondage. Why we do not has become the question at the center of my life. How did historical memory eclipse the extensive information about slaves and slavery that survives in the nation's vast repository of early documents? The hard question of how a post-Enlightenment nation founded on principles of personal liberty became the largest holder of slaves in the Western world is still before us, still waiting to be answered.

We need to try to find that whole history so that we can become a whole nation, one in which knowledge of the long story of people from Africa can begin to transform this country into a place of greater equality.

The answer to my friend's good question is that I am doing this because I find I cannot turn away from it. I am doing this because the lives of my father and mother led me here, to this history and to its exploration. I remember them and I remember Pegg, the enslaved woman who could not stop weeping.

With this book, I hope to honor them. This is my grief, for them and for this history.

The Logbooks

...le Imploy'd abo. rigging Carp. & Joiner making awning

...er Making a Pump Can — No Trade at all

...rday July 15th 1758 this 24 hours Light Winds & pleas. W...
...e Imploy'd ove hawling Blocks Carp.r & Joiner Making
...ng — No Trade only Bought Some Corn & plantins

...ay July 16th. this 24 hours Light Winds & pleas.t Wea.r People
...oy'd abo. Jobs Carp.r & Joiner abo.t the awning the Cap.t on
...d Wanton No Tra Purchased one boy Slave of Quaquom

...day July 17. this 24 hours Light Winds & pleas.t Wea.r Peo...
...loy'd over hawling tobacco Carp.r & Joiner abo.t the awning
...ade at all — Sail'd for Surrenam the Large Dutch S...
...500 & od Slaves onboard

...day July 18. this 24 hours Light Winds & pleas.t Wea.r People
...y in y.e Hold & fetching Brazeal Tobacco from a Dutc...
...Cap.t Buley — Purchased one man Slave

...esday July 19. this 24 hours Light Winds but a Large S...
...le Imploy'd picking Tobacco No Trade at all

...day July 20. this 24 hours Calm & little Wind People Imploy...
...Hold Cooper a Cutting Rum H.hd Purchased one Two Slave
...essels in y.e Rhode Except Three Poor Rum Men
...d the yaul up to Clean — broacht a bt Beef

...y July 20 this 24 hours Calm Weather People Imploy'd over
...ld & found a Hogs. N.o 86 Leaked all out N.o 85 only 54 Gal.s in b...
...gin to y.e Cap.t — Leakage oceationd by all y.e Head Hoops fly...
...ade this 24 hours — the agri'd with my Lord to Send a man
...to accraw after y.e Longboat for 4 Gal.s Trade Rum

...rday July 22d this 24 hours Calm Wea.r People Imployd fil...
...heads with Water & with Rum Cooper a Cutting Hogs...
...d from y.e Longboat by a Letter from Underwood w...
...y at Mumford with 3 Slaves on board

...day July 23d this 24 hours Calm & hazey Weather at 10.o
...y.e Ship to W. Ward which we Suppos'd to be the English Man of...

ONE

Recovering the Story

CLEARED FOR AFRICA

On a bitter January Monday in 1757, a ship called the *Africa* came to sail in the harbor of New London, Connecticut. Joshua Hempstead, who had been keeping a daily diary since 1711, wrote that January 17 was "fair & clear & very Cold."

The old man lived a stone's throw from the water, and might even have seen the *Africa* leave the harbor, but for a port as deeply involved in trade with the British Caribbean as New London, with a dozen or more ships "cleared out" or "enter'd in" from the West Indies every week, a single, Africa-bound ship probably didn't attract more than ordinary notice.

In his tiny cabin aboard the *Africa*, as the ship neared Long Island's Montauk Point the next afternoon, eighteen-year-old Dudley Saltonstall noted in his pristine new logbook the hour, the wind from the northwest, and the position of his ship on that first, bitter afternoon. It was his first entry.

Fair-haired and stocky, Saltonstall, though still a teenager, was aloof and proud. He was sailing aboard a ship owned by his father Gurdon, the deputy (a kind of mayor) of New London, a merchant of considerable means and the son of one of colonial Connecticut's early governors. The family was related to the Saltonstalls, Dudleys, and Winthrops, ruling families of the Massachusetts colony since its founding. Both Dudley's surname and Christian name were those of governors.

John Easton of Middletown was master of the vessel, and at thirty-nine he had already served as commander on slaving ships for a decade. Dudley was aboard the *Africa* as Easton's right hand, and to serve as *supercargo*, a position in which he would watch over the ship's supplies and the labor of the seamen, and protect his father's interests on the voyage.

The two men, both descendants of New England's early settlers, were sailing their fast, two-masted ship on a voyage to Africa, guiding the 110-ton vessel in a long loop across the Atlantic Ocean and down more than 3,000 miles of the lush West African coast. They were sailing to windward, and following the prevailing winds to what was often called the Windward Coast. These winds blew in a clockwise direction, and it was the most natural way to go. Though not an easy voyage—a reliable way to measure longitude was still decades away, and it was hard for mariners to know exactly where they were on the Earth's ocean surface—it was familiar to Easton, and a learning voyage for Saltonstall. (Inside the front cover of his logbook, Saltonstall wrote the rules for figuring course and distance using a trigonometric formula that was standard for the time. He also wrote what appears to be a practice equation.)

Saltonstall and his commander were sailing to West Africa to buy slaves and then to sell them on England's colonial islands in the Caribbean. A small number of their human cargo probably returned with them to New England. Easton and Saltonstall were part of what today we call the Atlantic world of the eighteenth century. Easton was already what the teenaged Saltonstall would become: a full participant in the system of trade that made New England rich and powerful, and made the Caribbean black.

This trade system made America not only dependent on the wealth that derived from slavery, but also a society that held slaves. The two Connecticut men were part of a history that transformed the Western

Hemisphere, even as it solidified their own wealth and prosperity. The dark and terrible core of that history, one that has not been integrated into the shared stories of early New England, is told in the logbooks that Dudley Saltonstall began to keep on that January afternoon and continued to keep for three voyages made in the twenty months that followed.

Like the insect that no longer exists anywhere on Earth but is frozen in a fragment of amber, the eighty handwritten pages of Saltonstall's logbooks offer a perfectly detailed glimpse of a now-distant past. They are an emissary from the past, proof of a past that really happened, that had material substance. The logbooks are not just an idea but a powerful form of evidence. They are a history that was lived and then lost, and is our very own.

SHADOWS ON THE WALL

We are who we are because of what we learn
and what we remember.
ERIC KANDEL

More than twenty years ago, scholar Arna Alexander Bontemps, son of Harlem Renaissance writer Arna Bontemps, began to explore an intriguing and troubling aspect of documents surviving from the first two centuries of Southern slavery. He found that in the early personal records of Southern slaveholders, slaves generally appear only in terms of purchases, or as laborers, as in "Mulatto Jack arrived from Fredk With 4 Beeves," or "Colo. Bassetts Abram arrivd with Letters from his Master."

As human beings with varied personalities, as participants in the household, as people with diverse skills, captives were rarely part of the record. Bontemps found many examples, including that of a plantation owner whose account of a fierce lightning storm that struck his mansion emphasized the fear it aroused and its awesome power, rather than the three enslaved men who were struck by the lightning and nearly killed. Slaves appeared in the record as a reflection of wealth, or as workers. Otherwise, they were a shadowy presence, "seldom unseen," Bontemps writes, "but judged by the way in which they were most often portrayed, they were virtually invisible as subjects." As captives, their real selves could not be lived openly.

This reality pervaded a culture where enslaved labor was already essential. Essential, and yet not seen. When I began to study New England slavery in the spring of 2002, I was baffled. Despite a wealth of books documenting the extent, character, importance, and influence of slavery in America, as well as a vast archive of original documents substantiating its nature, slavery is rarely taught in schools, and our understanding of its scope is barely rudimentary. The mainstream of American thought still does not contain a shared body of information on slavery even though the facts about American enslavement are widely available. Several years after that first spring, when I began to speak publicly about the book that had come forward from a newspaper project on slavery in the North (*Complicity*), I was asked the same question over and over, by audiences around the country: "Why don't we know about this?"

I thought that something else had to be at work for this narrative failure, something that touched on shame and reluctance but was larger than those, something that was also involuntary. Decisions get made about what gets remembered, but they are not all conscious ones. Scholars cautioned me to "contextualize" slavery, but I couldn't see what its context was. The truth I was trying to get at had a frayed, eroded quality, as if its damage had begun a long time ago.

The problem is not one of material but of memory, and not only of the history we have, but of how that history was made. What is missing from our history of slavery is the context for integrating, in a broad way, what we were thinking and how we were thinking when we made ourselves not just a nation that held slaves, but the largest slaveholding nation that had ever existed. And the questions that are right behind "Why don't we know about this?" are as important: "Why does it matter for today, and what would such knowledge change?"

The incomplete narrative of American slavery cannot be made whole without a reframing of our early history. The black "invisibility" that Bontemps found in Southern records permeates Northern documents as well; there too, black men and women appear mainly as possessions and as workers. Essential yet held in the shadows.

Adam mowed the Little pasture before the Door & Stacked the
   oats.
Adm Carted 3 hhd [hogs head barrels] for a west India man
   from Colln Saltonstalls to Ms. Shackmaples.

The year before I began to explore the story of slavery in New England, my mother was diagnosed with dementia, an illness that causes

the brain to forget what it holds, and that makes even the deeply familiar unrecognizable. As I looked for ways to help my mother, we stum-
bled together over the terrible terrain of her last years. There was a
moment when I realized, with the force of a blow, that she would never
recover, never get her memory back, never return to me and be my
mother. But the story of those Connecticut slave ships and their captains, *that* story, I could recover.

CREATING A RECORD

In the pages of his atlas-shaped logbook, Dudley Saltonstall carefully ruled off spaces for the information he was to record every two hours. In a flowing and legible hand, he wrote the name of his ship, his commander, their home port, and their destination across the top of every set of facing pages. He noted the day, the hour, the speed at which the ship was traveling and its course, as well as the direction of the wind and the nautical miles traveled. Under "Transactions," Saltonstall described the weather and made a few notes on what happened aboard the ship each day.

Later commissioned one of the first captains in the Continental Navy during the Revolutionary War, the young ship's officer kept track of how much food and water was brought aboard the ship and when the barrels of food and water were "broacht." The men ate beef, pork, mackerel, and mutton, all salted, as well as a hard cracker called "ship's bread," and potatoes.

The crew would have been small, probably not more than eight men. Saltonstall noted in his log the tasks at which the men were employed throughout the day. Subject to the worst hardships of shipboard life as well as the dangers of the slave trade, these seamen were from the lowest ranks of colonial life, and they were driven hard. A neighbor of mine who was an expert on maritime history read the logbooks and said, "You wouldn't have wanted to give these men too much time to think." On the coast of Africa, a seaman named Denis Bryan would try to desert but was captured on shore and brought back to the ship in chains.

English commander John Newton, who served as master on three slaving voyages to the same stretch of African coastline and during the same decade as Easton and Saltonstall, wrote that the world of the slave ship was one governed by harsh practice, and that "a savageness of spirit, not easily conceived, infuses itself into those who exercise

In.³ The Africa John Easton Coman...

Day	H	K	½	Course	Winds	Transactions
	2	4	1	SSE	NW	Tuesday Jan.º 18. 1757
	4	4	1			on the 17 Ins.t at 8 AM Came
	6	4				to Sail in the Harbour of N...
	8	4	1			Wind at NNW; at Meridian
	10	5			N	Montoh: in the Latt.º 41:18
	12	5				& Long 70:20 W.th Bore Was...
	2	4				Distance 3 Leagues
	4	4	1		N E	
	6	5				Fresh Wind & very Coul...
	8	5			N	
	10	6				Broacht 1 bb. Pork & 1 b...
	12	6		118 mile		Mutton

Course	Distance	D. Lat.º	Dep.ʳ	Latt Yᵖ	D. Long.º	Long in	M Course
S S E	116 mile	1:47 S.	0:44 E	39:31 N	0:57 E	69:23	44...

Day	H	K	½	Course	Winds	Transactions
	2	5	1	S B E	N	Wednesday Jan.ᵍ 19. 1757
	4	5	1			Fresh Gales with Snow &
	6	6	1			Hail
	8	8				B.t Top Sails
	10	7	1			Hard Gales & very Cold
	12	7	1		N E	
	2	7	1			
	4	7	1			
	6	7				
	8	6				
	10	6				
	12	6		160 mile		

Course	Distance	D. Lat.º	Dep.ʳ	Latt Yᵖ	D. Long.º	Long in	M Course
S B E	161 mile	2:37 S	0:51 E	36:54 N	0:39 E	68:44	75...

Logbooks, Courtesy of the Connecticut State Library

Day	H	K	H	Course	Winds	Transactions
						Thursday Jan.ʸ 20. 1757 —
	2	9		SSE	NE	Small Breises with
	4	9				Squals of Snow —
	6	3				a Tumbling Sea
	8	3				Small Wind & thick Weaʳ
	10	3				
	12	3				
	2	3				
	4	3				
	6	3				
	8	3				
	10	0	1			Light Breses
	12	0	1			
		62 mile				

Course	Distance	D:Latᵒ	Depᵗ	Lat̃ :pã	D:Long	Long in	Mer: Dis
S12E	62 mile	0:57.S	0:24.E	35:57:N	0:29.E	68:15.E	99:E

Day	H	K	H	Course	Winds	Transactions
						Friday Jan.ʸ 21 1757 —
	2	2	1	SBW	SEBE	Small Winds & Clear Weaʳ
	4	2	1	S	ESE	
	6	3		SSW		Stᵈ to the Norᵈ
	8	2	1	NE	SE	Reifᵈ Top Sails fresh Gales
	10	3	1		SSE	Hove at 2 Pm
	12	4				Hove too under Fᵗ Sail
	2	2	1			Drift NE
	4	2	1			More Modᵗ made Sail
	6	4				Fresh Gales with Rain
	8	4				
	10	4				
	12	4				

Course	Distance	D:Lat	Dep	Lat:pa	D:Long	Long in	Mer:Dis
N:52:E	47 mile	0:29 N	0:38.E	36:26:N	0:47.E	67:28	137:E

power on board an African slave-ship." A slave ship was, in every sense and for nearly all on board, an oceangoing prison.

The ocean crossing could have been narrated by Captain Jack Aubrey, the hero of Patrick O'Brian's maritime novels. The *Africa* weathered wild seas, blizzards, and gale winds. The heavy longboat, to be used for trading ashore, tipped over in its chocks and had to be righted; that same January day, a seaman named Waterman got his hand caught in the mainsail's block and tackle, and his fingernails were torn off.

But by the second week of March, Saltonstall was recording visits to slaving outposts on islands near the African coast. He sent ashore 187 feet of New England white oak and eight casks of rum to the governor of St. Jago, the largest of the Cape Verde Islands and a major center for the slave trade. This gift was a gesture of generosity, one designed to open the way for trading. Like enslavement itself, the slave trade rested on a system of extreme violence, but it had its social conventions, and successful traders observed them.

Captain Easton went ashore with the gifts but returned, discouraged, and reported that trade was not to be had on terms he regarded as reasonable. An Irish trader who lived on the coast of Sierra Leone and knew Easton during the 1750s said the Middletown man grew impatient if a deal couldn't be made quickly.

The *Africa*, a ten-year-old Connecticut-built ship of Dutch design called a *snow*, was a slaving ship at the very height of the international slave trade, which lasted from the late fifteenth century until the last decades of the nineteenth—nearly 400 years. Of the estimated 12.5 million Africans sold into slavery in the Americas, more than half were sold between 1701 and 1800, and of that 52.4 percent, tens of

opposite:
Capt. Easton sent ashore 187 feet of white oak boards and eight gallons of rum as a gift for the governor of the slave trading center at an island off the African coast, but wasn't able to establish terms for trade. Logbooks, Courtesy of the Connecticut State Library

54 Day	H	K	1/2	Course	Winds	Transactions
	2				12 0 at Boards	Sunday March 13th 1757
	4					Sent 187 feet Oak Boards & 8 Gal.
	6					Rum a Shore for the Govener
	8			Came to Sail Wind	N.E.	at 6 AM Capt Easton came a Board
	10	5	1	S E b S 1/2 S		& found Little hopes of Trade to
						be had on Reasonabl Terms So
	12	5	1	—	at 8 och	thought Best to Sail for the Eolifsa
	2	5	.	—		at AM hove up our Anchor &
	4	5	.	—		Came to Sail for the Eolesses
	6	5	1	—		Took my Depn from Port Depray
	8	5	1	—		the head harbour of St Jagoes Islgtho
	10	6	.	—		Latt 15.0 No Long 22:56 W
	12	6	.	—		Brockt a Tiirse Bread
		88 mile				Latt pObs: 13:36 No

Course	Distance	D. Lat.	Dep.	Latt Made	D Long	Long in	Mer. Dij
S S E 1/2 E	88 mile	1:24 S	0:45 E	13:36 N	0:47 1/2 E	22:9 W	45:00 E
	2	6	S E 1/2 E	N N E	Munday March 14 1757
	4	6	—		Fresh Breisy & Hazey —
	6	6	—		
	8	6	—		
	10	6	—		
	12	6	—		
	2	5	1	—	
	4	5	1	—	
	6	5	.	—	
	8	5	.	—	Carpenter at work on Great Box
	10	5	1	—	people Scraping Quarter Decks
	12	5	1	—	
		136 mile			Latt pObs: 12:9 No

| S S E 1/2 E | 136 mile | 1:26 S | 1:45 E | 12:10 N | 1:48 E | 20:21 | 130 E |

thousands more were sold during the second half of the eighteenth century than during the first.

The slaving fortresses south and east of Sierra Leone, in what today is Ghana, have become more famous than the stretch of coastline where Easton and Saltonstall began their trading voyage aboard the *Africa*, but the Windward Coast was the one that slave ships would encounter first in their voyage, so it appears often in narratives of mariners and other visitors.

Research on the demographics of slavery—how many people were taken from which region, in what time period, and where they were sent—has made significant advances in the past few decades, and a database of the transatlantic slave trade has been built by scholars from England and the United States. Constantly updated with information from museums, university scholars, and period documents that come to light, the database contained in mid-2013 approximately 35,000 voyages, which its creators estimate may be 80 percent of all voyages made. From the Sierra Leone region, which in Easton and Saltonstall's day included parts of what are now Liberia, Senegal, Guinea, and Guinea-Bissau, an estimated 400,000 to 500,000 captives were taken.

Between 1751 and 1775—almost precisely the span of John Easton's career as a slave ship captain—more Africans were sold into slavery than during any other period of the entire transatlantic slave trade. The accepted estimate is that during those twenty-four years, 63,000 people were sold out of Africa every year, or, to use the slavers' expression, "sent off from the coast."

The competition to buy healthy men, women, and children was fierce, and the literature of the slave trade is full of the bitter complaints of captains who felt they were being cheated by the black traders and English agents, although the captains also were trying to get the most for the least. On this first voyage in the logbooks, John Easton was assembling a human cargo destined for sugar plantations on St. Kitts, a Caribbean island with rich soil, heavy rainfalls, and cool temperatures. Sugar had been, at that point, cultivated on the island for more than a century.

As was customary for many slave ship captains of that time, Easton "slaved" his ship in a very deliberate way, but not from any single source. Saltonstall noted slaves being rowed out to the *Africa* for inspection and possible purchase, and the captain going ashore at the beachfront outposts of black traders where groups of potential slaves had been brought for sale and were held in filthy pens.

Easton also pursued the more dangerous slave-gathering method of going ashore in the longboat and navigating the crocodile-filled African rivers that were lined with independent traders who were black, white, and mulatto. "Boating," as it was called, exposed the captain and the seamen who accompanied him to being cut off from the ship, killed, and having their trade goods stolen. English muskets were a prime article of trade, and at this point in the commerce of slavery, both the traders from ships and the traders onshore were armed.

More than thirty years earlier, in 1726, British cartographer William Smith was commissioned to make a full report of the slaving operations, people, wildlife, and trade on the Sierra Leone coast, and he saw an armed Africa up close. "No sooner had [the chief mate] left me, and got out of Sight, and Call, but I was quickly surrounded by the savage Natives, who were all arm'd, either with Javelins, Bows, or Poison'd Arrows, or European Guns."

Easton had acquired twelve captives, five of them children, but trade was still slow when Saltonstall noted on the sixth day of April that they were "under Sail bound for Serrelone."

Sierra Leone, a country on the upper western coast of Africa, had been known as a center friendly to ships and trade since the mid-sixteenth century, when Englishman John Hawkins, a dashing adventurer and favorite of Queen Elizabeth I, stopped there to trade for captives—also taking them by force from foreign vessels where they were already held—and to fill his casks with the fresh water that flowed out of the mountainsides.

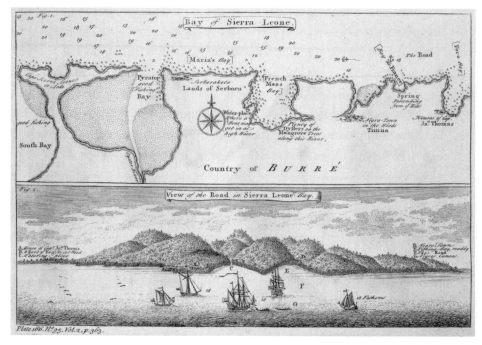

Sierra Leone became a locus of the slave trade in the sixteenth century, when English adventurer and mariner John Hawkins, a favorite of Queen Elizabeth I, seized Africans, made them captives, and shipped them to Hispaniola. Visitors to the country, which was named by the Portuguese for the mountains that looked like reclining lions, often remarked on the beauty of its coastline. From the author's collection

By the mid-1750s, Europeans had been trading in Sierra Leone steadily for a century, and since the 1670s, there had been a slaving fortress on a small island situated near the mouth of the Sierra Leone River. The island had different names at different times, but was always a slaving enterprise. On old French maps, it sometimes appears as a tiny dot with the words "Fort Anglais," or English fort. Because I first saw the name as Bence Island, that is what I call it, though it was called Bance Island during the late eighteenth and nineteenth centuries and today is called Bunce Island.

In 1726 cartographer Smith described the beautiful bay that Easton and Saltonstall saw before making their way upriver to Bence Island in 1757. "The next Morning, we found ourselves in a small pleasant Bay, surrounded with exceeding high Hills, all cover'd with tall beautiful Trees, swarming with various Kinds of Birds, which, as soon as Day broke, made the Woods ring. . . . In this Bay is extraordinary good fresh Water, which, gushing out of the Rocks on the Side of the Hill, comes down like a Spout, so that we could fill all our casks."

By the time Easton and Saltonstall anchored the *Africa* in Frenchman's Bay, an inlet in what is now Freetown Harbor near a point of land called Cape Sierra Leone, a clock began to tick. This invisible but very real clock had begun ticking when the ship reached Sierra Leone, and it had a death's head painted on its face.

In a trade rife with lethal aspects, the slave trade also faced a natural deadline. The rainy season, which began each May and lasted until late October, made that part of the African coast almost unnavigable because of the high waters. A ship that stayed more than six months on the coast of Upper Guinea faced increasing losses. Crewmen and officers fell to malaria and yellow fever, the suffering of the captives already in the hold increased and their health worsened—rendering them a loss to the owners—and supplies of trade goods were exhausted. A crew decimated by disease and desertion was less able to maintain control over the ship's human cargo, who frequently fought back against their captivity.

Easton and Saltonstall appear to have moored the *Africa* near a tiny island called Plantain and set out for the fortress at Bence in the longboat they had christened the *Pompy*. The shifting sandbars of the Sierra Leone River are famously treacherous, and Bence, situated about eighteen miles upriver, is at the limit of navigation for even small ships. It was safer to navigate the archipelago of slaving islands in a small vessel, with a black pilot hired at Cape Sierra Leone. It was also at this point on April 11 that a seaman named Denis Bryan appears to have had enough of the slaving trade. He was probably one of the men rowing the longboat to and from the fortress, because he attempted to desert from the Pompy at 11:00 that morning, but Saltonstall reports that "[we] catcht him & Put him in Irons & Sent him in the Pompy to the Plantins [Plantain Island] where the *Africa* lay."

With Easton's permission, Saltonstall boarded a smaller vessel, a sloop called the *Good Hope*, which was anchored at Bence. For the next week, Saltonstall wrote in his log that the ship was lying at Bence Island "Taking in Slaves Wood & Water." He was to sail with the *Good Hope*'s commander, Alexander Urqhart, to the Caribbean island of St. Croix via St. Christopher's with a cargo of 169 slaves. Saltonstall may have changed ships because of his health. He mentions having a "fitt" aboard the *Africa* and dislocating the right side of his jaw. Medical attention would have been readily available on St. Christopher's, which was a popular port of call for New London mariners, second only to Barbados. Saltonstall also mentions having fits during the last of the three voyages in the logbooks, one so severe that he lost consciousness.

Easton's destination was also St. Christopher's, or St. Kitt's as it is called today, but the commander evidently thought the prices for captives at Bence Island too high, and he headed south and east to Cape Coast Castle, an English trading fort on what was then called the Gold Coast and today is Ghana. Cape Coast Castle—which figures largely in the last slaving voyage in Saltonstall's narrative—was, in effect, Great Britain's home office for its slave trade in Africa for nearly a century and a half. A large fortress perched on rocks above the South Atlantic, Cape Coast would have been perfectly familiar to a captain with Easton's experience, and he would have sailed its waters like a road. Indeed, the navigational pathway in front of this and other trading centers was often called, simply, "the Rhode."

The information that survives about the rest of the *Africa*'s voyage is that the ship reached St. Kitts the following December with 100 slaves to disembark. John Easton had been at sea for nearly eleven months. British custom at the time was for a vessel to carry several slaves for each ton of the ship's capacity, though this practice was not law and was frequently disregarded in favor of "close packing" of slaves. The length of Easton's time on the African coast and the low per-ton ratio—100 captives in a 110-ton vessel—suggest that this was not a profitable voyage, but one that he drew to a close to preserve the lives already on board. (According to an earlier record, Easton landed his 100 captives in Jamaica.)

Dudley Saltonstall, who would later serve as master of the *Africa* and later still be held responsible for the greatest maritime disaster of the American Revolution and one of the sorriest episodes in American naval history, took his logbook with him and left the *Africa*. As the pages in the logbooks show, he was about to sail into a nightmare.

At 7:00, the hour on an August night when light begins to fade, my mother turned in her narrow bed and peered up into my face. I knew she was trying to place me. Some days, I was her sister, a college-educated secretary who had died young. Other days, I was her mother, a punishing woman who had died twenty-five years earlier and to whom my mother still wrote every week, despite her illness, to apologize for being out of touch. Mama would write the address of her childhood home on the envelope.

"Am I alive?" she often would ask me, trusting that the tall, white-haired woman at her bedside, a woman who was familiar in a way she could not describe, would be able to tell her. I had expected her to forget who I was, but had not understood that she would also forget who *she* was.

Without a stable memory of the events of her long life, with neither a past nor a future, she drifted in the present, each day seeking a coherent explanation as to who she might be. Without a personal history to center her and give her purpose, she began her utterly unfamiliar life over again every day in the supervised residence she called, simply, "the place." She was always surprised that I knew where she lived, asking, "How did you find me?"

We could no longer share family stories because I was from a family she did not remember, so I talked to her about my research into the history of New England and slavery. I told her about my work on a set of eighteenth-century ships' logs that held a long-submerged piece of the Connecticut story.

Before dementia, in the life when she played Chopin and read all the books for my college English courses, my mother had loved history. Sitting on the edge of her bed that August evening, I explained to her that the names in the ships' logs had led me to old newspapers, probate inventories, and land records, and that in those old documents I found other men and other ships linked to the slave trade in Africa. I told her that a professor from Connecticut College had called one morning to say, "I hear you found the smoking gun."

"I am going to Africa to see the island where the man who kept the ships' logs bought slaves," I said to my mother, explaining that I needed to see the island and walk in its ruins, and to stand where human beings had been bought and sold. I told her that the island had been abandoned for two centuries, and was considered a haunted place.

I didn't want to frighten her, but to include her in my work, as she had been included when she was well. These ships had sailed from a colonial port whose history had always fascinated us both. On a day when I had first read in the logbooks of children being purchased, I had had an olfactory and auditory experience so powerful that I forgot I was at a table in the state library and thought, for a long moment, that I was in Africa, seeing tiny black children as they were handed up into the ships from longboats that rode low in the water, gulls scream-ing overhead as the seamen reaching down to grasp small, smooth brown arms. When I told my mother about it, she murmured, as if heartsick, "Oh, those children."

Her beautiful eyes were wide, and the tree outside her window was just a shape in the darkness. She was trying to remember what I was telling her, sentence by sentence. She was hearing every word.

"Is it terrible?" she asked. "Are you afraid?"

le Imploy'd abo: Rigging Carp: & Joiner making Awning
r Making a Pump Can — No Trade at all

rday July 15th 1758 this 24 hours Light Winds & pleas: We
Imploy'd overhawling Blocks Carp: & Joiner Making
ng — No Trade only Bought Some Corn & plantins

ay July 16th this 24 hours Light Winds & pleas: Wea: People
'y'd abo: Jobs Carp: & Joiner abo: the awning the Cap: or
Wanton No tra Purchased one boy Slave of Quaquom

day July 17. this 24 hours Light Winds & pleas: Wea: Peo
'oy'd over hawling tobacco Carp: & Joiner abo: the awning
ade at all — Saild for Sirrenam the Large Dutch S
500 & 00 Slaves onboard

ay July 18. this 24 hours Light Winds & pleas: Wea: Peop
y in y: Hold & fetching Brazeal Tobacco from a Dutc
Cap: Buley — Purchased one man Slave

sday July 19. this 24 hours Light Winds but a Large S
le Imploy'd picking Tobacco No Trade at all

day July 20. this 24 hours Calm & little wind People Implo
Hold Cooper a Cutting Rum & hd Purchased one Two Slave
esely in y: Rhode Except Three Poor Rum Men
the yaul up to Clean _____ broacht a bl Bee

y July 21 this 24 hours Calm Weather People Imploy'd over
old & found a Hogs: No 86 Leaked all out No 85 only 54 Gal: in b
gin to y: Cap: — Leakage ocationed by all y: Head Hoops fly
rade this 24 hours — the agreed with my Lord to Send a Man
to accraw after y: Longboat for 4 Gal: Trade Rum

rday July 22d this 24 hours Calm Wea: People Imploy'd fil
heads with Water & with Rum Cooper a Cutting Hogs
d from y: Longboat by a Letter from Underwood
g at Mumford with 3 Slaves on board

day July 23d this 24 hours Calm & hazey Weather at 10
he Ship to W: Ward which we Suppos'd to be the English Man of

TWO

The Haunted Land

MEETING THE SLAVE TRADERS

I met John Easton and Dudley Saltonstall in the spring of 2004 when a friend sent me an article that had been published in the *Hartford Times* in 1928. He enclosed a brief note that said, "Thought of you." The article, printed out from microfilm, described the logbooks of three slaving voyages, bound together in a single volume.

The logbooks described two voyages from New London to West Africa, and one voyage from West Africa to an island in the Caribbean, all made between January 1757 and August 1758. The tone of the newspaper article, one of cheerful bonhomie and brave Connecticut mariners, was set by the first sentence:

> No Odyssey of the Old Connecticut shipmasters surpasses for romance and danger the bread-and-butter adventures of the Yankee slaver out of New London and the river towns. Bartering rum for Shylock's "pound of flesh," filling the wood-bin from the jungle and beating off "hi-jackers" to the trade with grape-shot, they raced back under canvas to American auction-blocks in the attempt to beat the spectre of death.

Despite the article's exaggerated air of derring-do, which was typical for the time, and the mistaken idea that most Africans were brought directly to the American colonies and "American auction-blocks," I was intrigued. The idea of Connecticut men commanding slave ships was new to me, despite my state's proximity to Rhode Island, which was colonial America's largest transporter of slaves to the Caribbean and the colonies. But no book or scholar during my earlier research had suggested such a possibility to me, so I had not looked for evidence of that commerce. *Not seen because not looked for.*

My friend had sent me the article because, at the time, I was working as a newspaper reporter at the *Hartford Courant* but on special assignment to write, with two colleagues, a book about New England's relationship with human enslavement before the Civil War and after. (The book was published in 2005 by a division of Random House.) I had been studying slavery in Connecticut and New England for almost two years, and knew that Rhode Island men were at the helm of 90 percent of the ships that brought captives to the American South, an estimated 900 ships. The ships always seemed to have pretty names: *Charming Susannah*; the *Swallow*; the *Greyhound*; the names of beautiful wives and beloved daughters, swift birds and virtues. Much later, I found Robert Hayden's poem about the Middle Passage, the sea voyage from Africa into the place of enslavement, and those dark ships, "their bright ironical names / like jests of kindness on a murderer's mouth."

In the course of researching, I learned that colonial Connecticut had been a major provisioner of the British West Indies plantations where slaves were growing and processing sugar in a monoculture that yielded huge profits to England. Connecticut-grown onions, potatoes, pigs, and cows were considered the best of the best on the Caribbean's English plantations, and the sturdy white oak we grew also was highly sought after. The horses raised on farms in eastern Connecticut were shipped to the Caribbean in the tens of thousands, and the colony's newspapers were filled with ads for "fat shipping horses." These advertisements usually displayed a chubby, prancing horse.

In the same way that sugar agriculture killed enslaved men and women—roughly one-third died in the first thirty-six months after arrival—it also killed the horses sent to plow the fields and turn the wheels of the sugar mills, many living just a single harvest. English settlers made an Eden-like Caribbean into a hell on earth for its enslaved black workers, and Connecticut livestock and produce supported what scholar Gary Nash called "the heartless sugar system."

When I studied the customs records of colonial Connecticut ships sailing to and returning from the Caribbean, and saw the newspaper advertisements for tropical products such as nutmeg and Madeira and "raizins," I understood that this was the broad record of human enslavement and suffering. The fortified wines and exotic spices were coming from a place where slaves were worked to death and then replaced because it cost less to import a life from Africa than to raise a child to slavery in the Caribbean. But I had not *felt* the information I was seeing.

In order to begin to understand, and to be guided by empathy and be changed, I had to cross the street.

I can explain.

The *Hartford Courant*'s offices are almost within sight of the Connecticut State Library, a massive gray block of a building where the ships' logs had been since their acquisition from the widow of a North Carolina collector in 1920. I showed the article to my editor at the newspaper, and she said, "Check it out." Jenifer Frank, who was editing our book as well as writing a chapter on New England's cotton connections, was deep into her own research and writing. A slender, intense woman with wildly wavy hair and a smile that transforms the severity of her bookish face, Jeni waved her hand at me and said, "Go, go."

The 250-year-old logs are fragile, and are stored in a temperature-controlled manuscript vault, so the librarian asked me to read them first on microfilm. Microfilm is hard to read, and as I tucked the end of the filmstrip onto the spool, I wondered if I'd find anything to bring back to Jeni, or if I would even be able to decipher the microfilmed pages of eighteenth-century handwriting. I worried that I didn't have enough background on the slave trade to understand what I would see.

Trance Actions on Board the Sloop Good Hope Alex.r Urquhart — Com.r

April 11th 1757. being Munday.
At 2 PM Took My leave of Cap.t Easton. & Came to Serrelone factory in the Pompy & took Passuage in the Sloop Good Hope, Alexander Urquhart Com.r bound to St Cruix via St Christophers at 11 PM Denis Bryan Deserted from the Pompy & at 12 AM catcht him & Put him in Irons & Sent him in the Pompy to the Plantine where the Africa Lay —

Teusday 12th April 1757
On Board the Good Hope Lying of the Factory at Bence Island. a Taking in Wood & Water &c.a —

Wensday 13th April 1757.
On Board the Good Hope Lying at Bence Island Taking in Rice Slaves Wood & Water —

Thirsday 14 April 1757. —
On Board the Good Hope Lying at Bence Island Taking in Slaves Wood & Water

Friday 15th April 1757. —
On Board the Good Hope Lying at Bence Island Taking in Slaves & Stores this Day J.t Dind & Suped at the factory with Cap.t John Stephens

Saturday 16.t April 1757. —
Lying at Bence Island Taking in Slaves & Water —

Sunday 17th April 1757. —
at 8 AM on Board & Came to Sail Bound Down Serrelone River at 11. Came to Anchor Near the Rocks — Spoke with a Schooner Belonging to Rhode Island M.r Cloude Com.r from the Benajoners Bound to Bence Island with 39 Slave on Board who T.d Cap.t Alex. Dondass from Gambe Bound to the West Indies with 150 Prime Slaves on Board: the ship was Cut of & all the Crew Put to Death Save the Carp.r & Boy & Run the Vessel a Shore at

Logbooks, Courtesy of the Connecticut State Library

Tranceactions on Board the Sloop Good

Munday 18.t April 1757.

Lying Near the Rocks till 8 AM Weig'd Anchor & Came
to Sail bound Down Serrelone River at Mer. Saw Capt.
Cason in a Sloop Lying at Anchor in frenemans bay —

Tuesday 19.t April 1757.

at 3 PM Came to Anchor in white Mans Bay at 8 Weighd
& Came to Sail Beating up to the Edless at 10 AM abrest of
Cape Serrelone abo.t 4 Leagus of ———— fresh Bresy

Wensday 20.t April 1757.

A Beating up to the Edless at 2 AM Had a heavy Turnado
of Wind & Rain, Stile abrest of Cape Serrelone at 6 Leagus of
Light Wind, & Clear Weather ————

Thirsday 21.t 1757.

Beating up to the Edless Saw a Sloop at Anchor, Stile in
Sight of Cape Serrelone about 8 or 9 Leagus of ——
Light Wind, & Clear Weather ————

Friday 22.t April 1757

at 4 PM Saw, the Edless Baring NW B N Dis. 8 Leagus at.
8 AM the Edless Bore NNW Dist 6 Leagus
Light Winds, & Clear Weather ————

Satturday 23 April 1757

at 4 PM Came to Anchor at the Edless & Sent the Boat
a Shore for Water — & Brought George Doudle aboard

Sunday 24.t April 1757

Lying at the Edless Geting Wood & Water aboard —
a few of the Slaves Not very Well

Munday 25.t 1757.

at 4 PM Came to Sail bound to St. Christophers
at Merd.n in Sight of the Edless Baring S.o 5 Leagus Dis.t
Small Bresy, in about 9 fatham Water ————

The basement study room at the Connecticut State Library in Hartford was cool on that steamy May morning, and the tables were packed with genealogists and researchers working to reconstruct their personal histories. I looked at them, bent over their piles of books, and thought, *what am* I *looking for?*

The first shock of the logbooks was that the handwriting is easy to read. The log keeper's hand is relatively large and perfectly legible, and he made a distinctive "d" with the upright stroke of the letter curving to the left over the round part of the letter.

I started calling the narrator Sam, because the name Sam Gould is written in what looks like the same handwriting on the inside cover, and because the newspaper article in 1928 had referred to him that way. His spelling was highly phonetic—"sett" for *set*, "currant" for *current*, "breses" for *breezes*—but spelling was not then standardized in colonial America. Noah Webster's famous "Blue Back Speller," the first national attempt to standardize spelling and word usage, was still twenty-five years in the future.

The log keeper was clearly literate, and someone with authority. "In the Africa, John Easton Commander from New London Towards Africa" was written across the top of two facing pages of the first log. I knew that this could not have been John Easton's own log of the voyage, though he may indeed have kept one. But the handwriting, which seemed to be the same for each of three voyages, noted three different commanders. On a quick read through the logbooks, the organization of the pages, the language used, and the style of the notations all looked the same. A shipwright at Mystic Seaport and my neighbor who had researched maritime life both suggested that this was a private document, being maintained for someone else. The handwriting seemed to match the weather, and was sketchier when seas were rough. Many of these entries would have been written by the light of a guttering candle.

There were many entries I didn't understand. I didn't know why, as the ship neared Africa, crewmen were cleaning out the steerage, build-

When the ruins on Bence Island were rediscovered in 1947, part of the fortress still had a roof. Now, tall trees grow within the walls. Courtesy of Tom Brown/ *Hartford Courant*

ing an awning, and repairing the "carrages." What was "ricing" and "the factory" and a "panyar"? Later, I learned that all those terms are particular to a ship engaged in what was called then "the Guinea trade."

But on page 38 of what appeared to be the second voyage in the logbooks, the log keeper noted, on Wednesday, April 13, "On Board the *Good Hope* Lying at Bence Island Taking in Rice Slaves Wood & Water." Similar entries appear for the next three days. Though I was confused about many of the terms, and had no idea where Bence Island might be because it is so small that it does not appear on modern maps, I understood that "taking in slaves" meant trading for human beings and putting them on a ship. And I understood that this set of records could tell me information about the past in its very soul, at the moment this history was lived.

I was about to make a journey of my own, into these logbooks, and I would learn that of the dozens of slave castles that once dotted the

West African coast, tiny Bence may have sent as many or more Africans into Southern colonial slavery than any other slaving outpost. And then it vanished from the world's memory, the jungle claimed the tall walls of the fortress, and trees grew up in the roofless yards where captives were once held in the hundreds for sale. Even my tentative identification of the log keeper, as Samuel Gould, vanished and was replaced by more compelling evidence that surfaced and pointed to an aristocratic colonial named Dudley Saltonstall as the narrator of the tale.

On the other side of the Atlantic and a world away, New England's slavers and their ships did not become part of the history of American slavery, though they wrote some of its early chapters. These men would be described in their obituaries as West Indies merchants and sea commanders.

Their lost chapters, of which Dudley Saltonstall's logs are just one, are remarkable for what they contain, but remarkable also for what they illuminate about memory and its power. Working in an era when the slave trade was legal and often lucrative, Saltonstall and Easton would transform the suffering and enslavement of black people into beautiful things for themselves and their families. Neither would have felt he had anything to hide.

Nor did they need to worry. History and the workings of human memory would hide it for them. And in their story of commerce in Africa, I found a larger story and a way to think about American slavery. For almost eighty years, the logbooks sat on a shelf at the state library, waiting to tell their tale, waiting to serve as a symbol of New England's long forgetting. Their challenge to me has been to use them correctly and ethically in portraying a traumatic past.

Reformer Jane Addams once said that the first function of memory is to sift and reconcile. This, then, would be my work.

In the month when I first read the logbooks, I also found myself single
after twenty-five years in two long relationships, one of which had led
directly into the other.

Four years earlier, my father had died, and I was helping to care
for my mother, whose diagnosis of dementia had made it impossible
for her to live independently. It seemed like my whole life was about
the past, and about memory. I missed my father so acutely that I still
did not really believe he was dead, and every night drove home by the
building where he had worked during his career, as if I might see him
standing at his bus stop. My mother's steady decline cracked my heart
every day, and my job was all about a story New England seemed to
want to forget. I wondered how I had become, at fifty-three, so deeply
enmeshed in looking backward and in regret.

I fed a handful of quarters into the microfilm reader and printed out
a few pages of the logbooks documenting the purchases of slaves, and
took them back to the office of the Sunday magazine to show Jeni. I still
had everything to learn about the slave trade, and was sure only that
these pages showed people being bought by a man who had started his
journey in Connecticut.

Jeni looked at them, then up at me, and said, "Show Rob."

Robert Forbes, then on the staff of the Gilder Lehrman Center for
the Study of Slavery, Resistance, and Abolition at Yale University, had
mentored me through a newspaper investigation of Connecticut and
slavery and was helping me with our book. Rob is calm and patrician,
and wears beautiful tweed jackets; his late father was a scholar on porcelain. An authority on the Missouri Compromise, Rob likes to drive
and listens to garage bands in his car.

When I showed him the pages from the logbook, he leaped from
his chair. "Where did you get these?" he demanded, repeating, "Bence
Island! I can't believe this! Bence Island!" I had thought Rob might

already be familiar with the logs, but he had neither seen nor heard about them. And in the oddly novelistic way the story of these log-books was unfolding, it turned out that the world authority on Bence Island—a man who had spent almost thirty years studying the island and the eighteenth-century slave trade in the Sierra Leone River—was working in the next room but had just stepped out for lunch.

Joseph Opala takes his mealtimes seriously, and he was having a lei-surely lunch that day. I had eventually left Rob, and was piling books and notes into my car, when I heard Rob calling my name as he ran across the courtyard of the Gilder Lehrman Center building. His tie had blown over his shoulder, and he called "Come back! Joe's back!"

Joseph Opala, a faculty member from James Madison University in Virginia, had spent the spring semester at Yale on a fellowship drafting a plan for the stabilization of Bence Island and its eighteenth-century structures, which in their unprotected state are open to the elements and prey to theft. A strongly built Oklahoman with the ruddy com-plexion of a farmer and the nature of a contrarian, Joe had visited Bence at the end of a two-year stint in the Peace Corps in Sierra Leone during the mid-1970s. Trained as an anthropologist and interested in a past that is better measured in millennia than in centuries, Joe went to see the island simply as a courtesy to the American ambassa-dor. He found a beach covered with the undisturbed remnants of the eighteenth-century slave trade and ruins cloaked in thick vegetation. He also found a story that he could not leave, and in the ruins on Bence Island he found his Troy. He has researched the island's history for decades, and though forced to flee under a threat of death during the country's civil war, he returns several times each year.

Joe turned pale when he saw the logbook pages. "Do you have the rest of this?" he asked. "I thought I had seen *everything* on Bence Is-land, but I haven't seen this." My heart pounding, I said that I didn't have a copy of the rest of the logbooks, but that I would get one. Joe kept reading the few pages I'd brought, as if he could see more in them than was written there. He was breathing hard, and he walked in circles there in the office, while Rob beamed at him, at both of us.

I drove back to Hartford in an altered state. Something big had happened to me, *was* happening to me. I knew then that a door had opened, but I didn't yet understand that sorrow was written over its portal.

Six months after first seeing the logbooks on microfilm, I was on a plane to Belgium to catch a Swissair flight to West Africa. I had persuaded the management of my newspaper that a missing piece of Connecticut's history was lying on the ground on an abandoned island off the coast of Sierra Leone.

A photographer and videographer from the newspaper had gone over two weeks earlier to begin photographing and making film of Bence Island. Joseph Opala, who was to be our guide and translator, also had gone over early to hire men who lived on neighboring islands to clear the ruins of the fortress on Bence of their dense vegetation.

My friends at the newspaper asked how I'd persuaded our financially conservative paper to spend thousands on a story that happened 250 years ago. I could tell that many of them thought slavery was a story I needed to get over. The earlier investigation had been published two years before, and the book that followed was nearly finished. "Everything in Connecticut isn't about slavery," a columnist said to me, adding that his ancestors were nineteenth-century immigrants and had nothing to do with slavery. "Are you going to write about women?" a reporter asked. "Or how about modern-day slavery?" They were good questions, I knew, but nothing in my twenty-first-century life seemed as important as decoding these eighteenth-century ships' logs.

And the story of slavery was changing me. Those stolen people had suffered so long ago, and I could not find any place where their particular story was told. Who would speak for them, and why had a place not been made for them in our history? At our hands, they had been sold from the only home they knew into killing labor and suffering, and I was ready to do Jane Addams's memory work. I couldn't reconcile yet, but I was plenty ready to sift.

Though newspapers are portrayed in movies as freewheeling and democratic, they are, in my experience, intensely hierarchical and driven by favoritism. In terms of newsroom capital, I didn't have much. I had been working for New England newspapers for twenty-eight years, and at the *Hartford Courant* for more than half that time. I'd spent years writing and editing features about homes, gardens, and literary figures, and if people knew me at all, it was for a 1998 series that I'd written about what makes a marriage strong. It was my bad luck that a new editor in chief had joined the newspaper the week the series ran, and he was a hard-news junkie. He hated seeing soft stories on "One," and I heard that he had described the series at an editors' meeting as "longer than most marriages." The newspaper ombudsman wrote a column slamming it as a waste of precious page-one space.

I was nobody's idea of an investigative reporter. I was just grateful to be included, and I knew that when this project was done, I would probably be assigned to the home and gardening section, writing about crabgrass and hostess gifts. (Within months, I was.)

But in an odd moment of fate that was seeming less and less accidental, a group of lost black men, women, and children had come into my hands, and had made me responsible for bringing their story back. On that day in the library when I had the powerful waking dream of the children being handed up into the slave ship, I realized that I was crying, and a sympathetic genealogist across the table pushed a box of Kleenex toward me and said, "Your people?" And I thought, *they are.*

Both the captives and their captors began to appear at the edge of my dreams and followed me through the day. In a dream that recurred, I saw a slave ship leaving New London harbor, but I could not read the name on the transom as it sailed away from its anchorage. Looking down from the ship's high stern, a man in a long coat raised his three-cornered hat to me, and then looked out toward Long Island Sound.

I began to believe that something was guiding this project, and that it was not visible, or any part of Earth. From my friend sending me the news clipping, to the scholar who knew about Bence Island, to the newspaper's financial support of a backbencher with no reputation, a kind of divine intervention seemed to be at work. When I stepped off the plane in Sierra Leone's Freetown International Airport, and then waited for hours in a baking airplane hangar where sunlight poured in through hundreds of bullet holes in the tin roof, I knew I was lucky.

HISTORY FOR AN ABANDONED PLACE

And this also has been one of the
dark places of the earth.

JOSEPH CONRAD

From the air, Bence Island looks so small. It is hard to imagine the enormity of pain it has witnessed. Even when you are on the ground, the island feels small. Only from the water, in a small boat, does it seem to loom above you. The tall ruins of the last fortress, built in 1796 near the end of the island's long career as a depot for the slave trade, appear to be hiding amid the tall trees. They are there, and then not there.

Bence Island is visible from a hilltop near Fourah Bay College in Freetown, Sierra Leone's wracked and refugee-filled capital city. The island seems to curve within the protection of the vastly larger Tasso Island, which also formed part of the slaving archipelago centuries ago.

Early explorers often remarked on the beautiful haze of lavender and green that seems to envelop this part of the Sierra Leone River, and when I first saw tiny Bence in that lavender distance, I did not believe my eyes. The long and haunted story of that small place had become so deeply a part of me, and I had imagined it so often, that I could not believe I was finally seeing it from a hillside in Freetown, nothing between us except some air and water. I thought, *I have come so far for you.*

It felt like my body was full of tears. I could not bear to leave the hillside, even after Tom Brown, our photographer, and Alan Chaniewski, our videographer, had made their pictures and film.

In a series of letters published in 1788, John Matthews, a former British naval officer who was setting up a private business for trading in slaves on the Sierra Leone coast, described the harbor at Freetown and the river that leads up to Bence Island. It was what I saw, exactly.

Photographed from a hillside in Freetown, the capital of Sierra Leone, Bence Island is the small island in the center. The islands around it were part of a slaving
archipelago during the late seventeenth, eighteenth, and very early nineteenth
centuries. Courtesy of Tom Brown/*Hartford Courant*

"In coming in from the sea in the dry season, few prospects can ex-
ceed the Sierra-Leone river," wrote Matthews. "Before you is the high
land of Sierra-Leone rising from the Cape with the most apparent gentle ascent. Perpetual verdure reigns over the whole extent, and the
variegated foliage of the different trees, with the shades [shadows]
caused by the projecting hills and unequal summits, add greatly to the
beauty of the scene."

This part of Sierra Leone's coast includes equatorial jungle that
feels more dense than the densest New England forest. It is verdant
in a way that is hard for Westerners to imagine, and the air is so thick
it seems to lie upon your skin. Having grown up in mid-eighteenth-
century New London, Dudley Saltonstall would have been familiar
with a breeze off the harbor, stone houses, a white steepled church and
pasturelands; the African coast would have seemed like the shore of

Englishman John Matthews was planning to establish a slave trading business in Sierra Leone when he first saw the entrance to the Sierra Leone River. This engraving was published in his book *A Voyage to the River Sierra-Leone on the Coast of Africa*, late in the eighteenth century. Manuscripts, Archives, and Rare Books Division, Schomburg Center for Research in Black Culture, The New York Public Library, Astor, Lenox, and Tilden Foundations

another world, a distant latitude from the burnished leather globe in his father's study.

The next morning, we motored upriver in a small boat borrowed from the American Embassy. The eighteen-mile trip felt like an outing, the wind cool on my face because Gabriel, our pilot, kept the boat zipping along. This stretch of the river is filled with shoals and shifting sandbars, so ships in the era of the logbooks would have picked up a black pilot at a point of land in Freetown called Cape Sierra Leone, but in our light little boat we didn't have to worry. I admired the lush African coastline and the hills that come down almost to the water, and their gentle slopes. The coastline is punctuated with mangrove trees, which I had read about in the guidebooks of eighteenth-century visitors.

I felt as if I were inside the logbooks' first journey, seeing what the men on board the slave ships would have seen almost 250 years earlier: the sandy inlets, fallen trees lying in the water, white blossoms winding through végetation so thick it looked like a wall, and here and there a child, watching us from a small beach.

At 10:00 a.m. it was already nearly 100 degrees and steamy. Sierra Leone has a Muslim majority, and I had arrived during Ramadan, which is carefully observed in the isolated communities we were to visit. Out of respect to local practice and the Africans we met, I wore long sleeves and long pants, and covered my head with a scarf.

On the edges of the river as it grew wider, there were several clusters of old rusted structures that looked as if they might once have been parts of water towers and industrial cranes. I wondered how long they had been there rotting away; they emphasized the sense of emptiness and dereliction that seemed to hang in the sunny air. Much later, I learned that these structures are the ruins of a once-successful operation to move iron ore from a local mine through the deep-water port of Pepel Island. Corruption claimed the project in the 1970s, but the abandoned railways, conveyor belts, and company buildings are still on Pepel, lying in rust and ruin. In my dreams about Sierra Leone, they are always there at the side of the river.

A kind of fear stirred in me as we shifted course and our motorboat approached Bence, which spread before us horizontally. The tall ruins of the fortress are at the northern end of the island, and because they were only partially visible, I felt as if the ruins were watching me.

No one lives on Bence Island now. There was once a deep well, but there has never been electricity or running water. The island's caretaker, a slender Muslim named Braima Bangura, maintains a wedding-style scrapbook that he asks visitors to sign, but he lives with his family on neighboring Pepel. For safekeeping, he stores the scrapbook in a worn and scratched Ziploc bag.

The local people, many of whom are Temne, one of Sierra Leone's largest ethnic groups, believe the island is haunted, and will not stay

The sandy jetty where slave ships sent their longboats ashore and from which captive people were rowed out to ships from Europe and the American colonies is still perfectly visible. The ruins of the fortress are on a small rise to the left of the jetty, and hidden by trees. Courtesy of Tom Brown/*Hartford Courant*

here overnight. When daylight begins to fade, they drift back to their canoes, one by one. They believe that a devil sits on a rock just upriver of the island, and that he can stride across the water to come ashore. The belief is of very long standing, because I read of this devil in an account by an eighteenth-century Englishwoman who first came to the island in 1791. She called him the "old Gentleman."

I slipped down off the side of our boat and waded ashore, the water warm as a bath. The island has that particular silence of abandoned places, but as we walked onto the narrow beach, green monkeys began to scream from the treetops, and insects buzzed loudly. Something moved violently in a canopy palm. Mr. Bangura took my elbow gently, and made a wide gesture of welcome with his other arm, as if inviting me to Bence Island. I looked up at the small rise, a green pathway that leads up to the ruins.

The shore of Bence Island just below the ruins of the slaving fortress is still lit-tered with the detritus of the slave trade, including glass beads, cowrie shells, bits of clay pipes and stone ballast, and fragments of soft-paste porcelain such as this one. This might have been a piece of a plate or platter on which food was served to traders dining at the fortress. Courtesy of Tom Brown/*Hartford Courant*

    I suddenly felt terribly shy in front of my small team, and hoped they would not look at me. I could not say anything and did not want to make eye contact with anyone. I read later that this is how visitors to the death camps feel, but the only thing I felt at that moment was a sense of shame in having come to the island. The buoyancy I had felt at the airport was replaced by the feeling that the island's suffering history defied my pens and notebooks, and that I was in over my head. (At a college in New Jersey seven years later, a young African Ameri-can woman said to me, "Did you feel you had the right to just walk into our history?" and I understood that she was asking whether I had felt shame on that first day.) In my pocket, on a scrap of paper, I had writ-ten Saltonstall's words from the logbooks, "Lying at Bence Taking in Slaves Wood & Water," and I held that tightly as I followed Joseph Opala up to the entrance to the fortress.

I had seen film and photographs of the island in a documentary Joe had helped produce, but I wasn't prepared for how intact the fortress is. I had imagined piles of rubble and cairns that Joe would interpret, but in the same odd and unexpected way that the logbooks were perfectly legible, Bence Island was not hard to decipher. Its purpose, its layout, and its story did not have to be imagined. It was perfectly clear how the island had worked.

The jetty of stone and gravel that leads onto the beach is the same one that was used during the centuries of the slave trade. This is where the captives, with their arms roped behind them, would have been walked down to the longboats and pushed in. Though the trading of goods for each slave took place in a clearing just outside the fortress, the beach and the jetty are still littered with objects from the slave trade, two centuries after its end. I saw the stems and bowls of clay pipes no longer white but gray with age, and broken pieces of the porcelain transferware that the company agents and traders would have used when dining at the fortress. Brilliant ruby and azure beads of Venetian glass and cowrie shells, once used in payment for human lives, were thick on the ground, as were shards of old bottles. An eighteenth-century cannon, its surface pitted with age, lay on the jetty facing the river. A large old fragment of blue porcelain with the figure of a prancing horse shone in the grass near the water's edge.

On this jetty, a piece of slavery's story was lived and suffered. We accept the idea that time changes the layout of streets and waterfronts, and that, for instance, John Easton's wharf in Middletown no longer exists, and his stretch of riverfront is now a piece of a highway and a grassy verge. But this jetty was *that* jetty, the same one he and Saltonstall crossed; that sameness seemed to obliterate time itself. Seamen smoked their long clay pipes while men and women were shoved toward the longboats beached on the gravel shore. For most of those men and women and children, this small piece of land would have been their last moment on African soil, and though the place is now deserted and has the emptied-out atmosphere of a ruin, it is easy to imagine when it rang with commerce and the business it was about. The island was once a hive of activity, and its air, now so still, would have been pierced by shouts and cries.

We walked up to the clearing outside the main entrance. Joe explained that captives would be brought out from where they were held inside the fortress, and then examined for sale. For ten days before my arrival, men from nearby islands had been clearing the walls of dense vines and other vegetation so that we could make film and photographs of the ruins, and so that I could understand the layout. Joe had said that the fortress walls would tell me the story of what had happened here. Dark and rough with age, scabbed with tropical moss and lichen, the brick walls still have the power to frighten. These ruins are from the last slaving castle built on Bence Island, the last of perhaps as many as six fortresses, and was finished in 1796. The castle where Saltonstall and Easton traded in the 1750s was destroyed by the French in 1779. The fortress that followed that one also was destroyed by the French, but this last was, like all the others, built on the original site and the oldest footprint.

The exterior of the fort would have been covered with a white stucco that made the structure gleam, even from a distance. Made from ground white oyster shells, the bright stucco was not used on the inner walls of the slave yards, which were not for show.

Bence Island was a slave trading depot managed by Great Britain, the slave trade's international leader for centuries, so even though the island is a tiny place, it appears often in eighteenth-century reports, letters, and journals. As we walked on the island, I remembered fragments of the vivid accounts I had read.

Barry Unsworth, who relied heavily on the journal of mid-eighteenth-century English slave ship captain John Newton in writing his novel *Sacred Hunger*—Newton traded at Bence in the 1750s and lived on nearby Plantain Island for nearly a year—describes a slaving fortress that could only have been Bence Island: "On a rocky eminence above the river bank, rose the white fort, shimmering in the sunshine, dra-

Two centuries ago, the outer brick walls of the fortress on Bence Island were coated with a white stucco made locally of oyster shells. The white exterior was designed to impress, and the slave ships arriving for trade would have seen the fortress gleaming in the distance. Courtesy of Tom Brown/*Hartford Courant*

matic and imposing, with its block towers and high, crenellated walls. [The narrator] made out the Union Jack flying from the battlements, and another flag, blue and white—the colours of the Company."

Englishwoman Anna Maria Falconbridge was the first white woman to write an account of life in Sierra Leone during the late eighteenth century, the pivotal period when England began to move away from the slave trade. She visited the fortress that stood here in 1791 and 1792, and said it had a "formidable" appearance. "I suppose it is about one hundred feet in length, and thirty in breadth," she wrote in her memoir, "and contains nine rooms, on one floor, under which are commodious cellars and store rooms; to the right is the kitchen, forge, &c., and to the left other necessary buildings, all of country stone, and surrounded with a prodigious thick lofty wall."

As late as 1805, just before Great Britain withdrew from its position

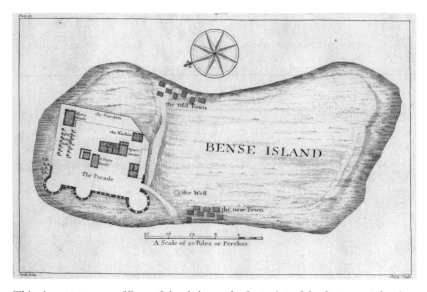

This circa 1727 map of Bence Island shows the footprint of the fortress at the time
when it was under the management of the Royal African Company of England.
When John Easton and Dudley Saltonstall visited the island in 1757, a consortium
of British and Scottish businessmen had been running the slave trading operations since 1748 and had made of them a great success. Drawing of Bence Island,
Sierra Leone, image Reference "Mariners 18," as shown on www.slaveryimages
.org, compiled by Jerome Handler and Michael Tuite, and sponsored by the Virginia Foundation for the Humanities and the University of Virginia Library

at the helm of the world slave trade and became one of the trade's most
ardent opponents, English traveler Joseph Corry visited the island and
wrote of its "elegant range of buildings and store-houses, which, with
great propriety, may be considered as one of the most desirable posi-
tions upon the windward coast of Africa."

Richard Oswald, a Scot, and Henry Laurens, an American from
South Carolina, made fortunes from the slave trade conducted here
but never set foot on the island. Oswald, head of a London-based consortium of merchants who leased Bence from the local African kings,
and Laurens, who bought hundreds of Sierra Leoneans to work on rice
farms in the American South, were traders on a global scale. They par-

ticipated in the slave trade with great success, but never felt this rocky shore under their buckled shoes or saw the towering mangrove trees. They never smelled the marshy stink of this earth.

In the logbooks and in the culture of the slave trade, this place was called, simply, "the factory." Saltonstall wrote on April 15, "This Day I Dind & Suped at the factory with Capt. John Stephens." (This is probably the same John Stephens, a slave ship captain, who worked directly for Oswald and his associates.) Substantial slaving outposts were often called factories, and their lead agents were called factors. These words remind me, always, that the slave trade was a business.

Company agents and military men came to Bence to manage the complex business of bringing captive people here from inland and hundreds of miles north and south of the island. The imprisonment, maintenance, and sale of those thousands of captive people also created work. There would have been accountants from England, and men who could build barrels and repair structures of wood and brick. There would have been white men and free blacks who plied the coastline in company vessels, scouting for captives to bring and sell at Bence. There would have been a doctor, though probably not a very good one. Sierra Leone's malarial climate was considered hazardous to whites, and at one time the country was nicknamed "The White Man's Grave." Bence Island, despite its popularity, many amenities, and success as a slave trading center, was a hardship post, and heavy drinking—drinking "away their senses," in trader John Newton's words—seems to have been part of daily life.

Forty years later, American slave trader Joseph Hawkins described the factors at an English slaving fortress south of Bence Island on the Rio Nunez by saying that as the day grew hotter, "The sacrifices to Bacchus commenced, with what they called a *whetter* before dinner. Some of our company, however, had been rather earlier at their devotions." Hawkins's description made me laugh, but I wondered, too, if being an agent of another's misery—or, in the case of traders and factors, the misery of hundreds and even thousands—in an environment as alien from Bristol, England, or Newport, Rhode Island, as one could find—would not lead to the kind of sustained drinking that erases guilt and feeling. A small glass of Madeira wasn't going to do it.

The main entrance to the fortress at Bence had an arched doorway, and beyond it I could see a large field.

In the month before visiting Sierra Leone, I had read of how the slaves were examined for sale. In 1721 the Royal African Company had sent a doctor named John Atkins to make a survey of all company holdings on the upper western coast of Africa, and to report on the slave trade, the customs of the tribal groups, and the life—both botanical and zoological—of the various regions of the coast. A surgeon in the British Royal Navy, Atkins also was to report on the slave trade in Brazil—he spelled it *Brasil*—and the West Indies. Atkins brought with him many of the prejudices common to an Englishman of his day, but he was an intrepid traveler, and had a keen eye.

He witnessed the "very dejected" condition of the captives being brought forth for sale at Bence Island and at the private traders on the shore just opposite the island's northern end. While there, Atkins saw a man given "an unmerciful Whipping," with a strap made from the rough hide of a manatee, for refusing to be examined by a trader. The man was a tribal leader who had already killed two slave traders, Atkins explained, and he would have been beaten to death except for his evident strength and courage, which had commercial value.

"He seemed to disdain his Fellow-Slaves for their Readiness to be examined," the surgeon wrote, "and as it were scorned to look at us, refusing to rise or stretch out his Limbs, as the Master commanded." The man bore his beating "with Magnanimity, shrinking very little, and shedding a Tear or two, which he endeavor'd to hide, as though ashamed of."

Sixty years later, Sierra Leone trader John Matthews described the way he saw trade conducted at Bence and other locations, and wrote that once the captive was carefully examined for imperfections, the traders got down to brass tacks. "If approved, you then agree upon the price at so many bars, and then give the dealer so many flints or stones to count with." Iron bars were a kind of baseline currency in the slave trade, and their value fluctuated in response to time, location, and supply. All commodities were valued in these bars—from rum, tobacco, and gold dust to cloth, muskets, and human beings.

The beach had been covered with rough-edged ballast stones and flints, too.

THE SCREAMING MAN

We walked into the large, brick-walled yard where the men would have been held, sometimes for many days, exposed to the heat and rain. The ground was rough, and patched with weeds and small trees. The sun felt merciless, and the surrounding walls were very tall, making the yard airless and chokingly hot. On a visit to the island in 1791, Anna Maria Falconbridge had strolled to the windows of Bance Island House, as the fortress was then called, and looked down into this enclosure from the cool upper room where she was about to enjoy dinner.

> Involuntarily I strolled to one of the windows a little before dinner, without the smallest suspicion of what I was to see;—judge then what my astonishment and feelings were, at the sight of between two hundred and three hundred wretched victims, chained and parceled out in circles, just satisfying the cravings of nature from a trough of rice placed in the centre of each circle.
>
> Offended modesty rebuked me for not hurrying my eyes from such disgusting scenes; but whether fascinated by female curiosity, or whatever else, I could not withdraw myself for several minutes—while I remarked some whose hair was withering with age, reluctantly tasting their food—and others thoughtless from youth, greedily devouring all before them; be assured I avoided the prospects from this side of the house ever after.

In the heat and silence, I felt as if I could not speak. Joe said, "What? No questions from the reporter?" But then he leaned toward me and, his voice gentle, said, "No one speaks here."

Months earlier, I had told my mother that I wanted to stand in the *barracoon*, or enclosure, where those men had been held. I looked up at the empty windows that open onto this barren and broken space, and wondered if Easton and Saltonstall, like Anna Maria, had stood in the upper rooms of earlier fortresses and looked down.

By the time he visited Bence Island in 1757, John Easton had already built a large, gambrel-roofed house on the Connecticut River, and he owned a wharf and livestock. He must have loved beautiful things—silver swords, English furniture, a "delph" platter and "chocolate bowles"—because his will and property inventory, written in 1770, document twenty closely written pages of possessions, the kinds of things you see in New England historical societies and museums. The merchant Richard Oswald, who participated in the slave trade on a much vaster scale than Easton and probably would have found the Middletown man provincial, had a castle on a river in Scotland, and collected landscapes and paintings with religious themes. He owned Scotland's first greenhouses, where he grew sugar cane, fig trees, and exotic plants; Robert Adam, the great Scottish architect, designed a teahouse for Oswald in the shape of a miniature castle complete with turrets.

To enter the slave yard, we had walked through a double doorway once used by the *grommetos*, who were free black workers employed by the company to serve the interests of the trading post. They repaired ships, managed company vessels along the coast, and grew food for the fortress and for trade ships like the *Africa*. They carried in food and water to the captives and brought out the buckets of human waste, passing under an armed guard positioned on the wall above the double doorway. There was no way for a captive to escape, for even if he managed to escape the enclosure, there was an outer fortress wall that was locked and guarded. The island waters swarmed with crocodiles, and the neighboring islands also were leased to Oswald's company, so there was no refuge there either.

There was a smaller, separate enclosure where the captive women and children were held, and this was adjacent to the barracoon. The inner and outer walls of this enclosure are partially intact, but the roof that it once had is gone. Scholars estimate that women and children comprised about one-third of the total number forced into New World slavery.

The service entranceway to the enclosures where captive men, women, and children were held for sale is a double doorway, with one door diagonally behind the other to discourage the possibility of escape. These two doorways would have been guarded by a man with a gun. Courtesy of Tom Brown/*Hartford Courant*

Tribal people were brought from many different locations in the interior and from along the coast to be sold at Bence, and often, by the time they reached the island, they had passed through the hands of several traders. The purpose of the transatlantic slave trade was to acquire labor, and in the functioning of this trade, black people were separated from their home villages and from one another. James Stanfield, who had served aboard slave ships and then later regretted his actions, wrote to British antislavery advocate Thomas Clarkson and scoffed at the notion that slaves were the spoils of intertribal wars: "I am inclined to think, that the method of collecting slaves by war, dreadful as that mode may be, is by no means the great support of the Slave trade: but that they are procured by the still more infamous and horrid practice of *kidnapping.*"

A trader might buy the mother and not the children, or the husband and not the wife. In the same way that enslaved families in America were often separated and sold away from each other, their ancestors had been separated and sold in Africa. First mentioned to me by Joseph Opala, this interruption of kinship systems is a natural function of the way the slave trade placed the greatest value on young, able-bodied men. Young, healthy women of childbearing age also were valued, but there was no advantage for traders to keep African families intact.

The people held on Bence Island would have been disoriented and frightened. They would have heard languages they had never heard before, and they might have been hungry and exhausted. Many of the captives were brought from inland Sierra Leone, as well as from inland regions of what today are Liberia and Guinea, and they would never have heard the wash of surf. They would never have seen anything like the Bence Island fortress, and might never have seen white faces before. (On Tasso Island later in my trip, a playful woman pulled off my headscarf. Her toddler had burst into tears at the sight of me, with my pale skin and white hair.)

The shouted commands, brutal examinations, guns, and beatings also communicated a message to the captives, even though they did not understand what was being said. Standing in the enclosure, I felt a chill underlying the dense heat and wondered if there exists a kind of terror so great that it can become part of a site and make it forever a place apart, suitable only for prayer and remembrance.

The black traders working along the rivers and coastline would have understood that the captives were destined for lives of hard physical labor because the greatest demand was for adult men; but even these African traders, functioning against their fellow Africans, would never have seen a Caribbean sugar plantation, or a Carolina rice farm, or a New England village, all places where captives lived and suffered.

In his book-length account of English trade in Africa, Brazil, and the West Indies, surgeon John Atkins wrote sympathetically, "To remove *Negroes* then from their Home and Friends, where they are at ease, to a strange Country, People, and Language, must be highly offending against the Laws of Justice and Humanity; and especially when this change is to hard Labour, corporal Punishment, and for Masters they wish at the D[evi]l."

And although the captives knew very little for certain, they knew enough to be afraid. By the time they reached Bence, they had already been separated from their home villages, which was a kind of death. When I saw the carefully maintained graves of long-ago chiefs, and was, at every turn, introduced to the oldest people in the villages we visited, I understood that the tribal people of two and three centuries ago would never have left their homes, and that the slave trade interrupted sacred spiritual and domestic connections. To lose one's community was to lose everything that mattered.

The people held aboard ships often attempted to revolt against their captors, or tried to commit suicide by starving themselves or jumping overboard. The captives could not imagine their fate, but they probably knew, as did their jailers and captors, that they were never coming back.

When we visited Tasso Island the first time, a young, handsome village leader in a long parrot-green robe offered to buy me. When he offered twenty cows for me and the translator explained that I was a fifty-cow woman, everybody chuckled; his offer was understood to be not a real one, but simply a compliment from a younger man to a woman twice his age. Only much later did it occur to me that an offer to buy me—in essence, to capture and *own* me—was an odd and chilling joke in a culture where enslavement had once been the norm.

The most perfectly intact portion of the ruins on Bence is the powder magazine, a descending walled passageway that we entered from a hole in the earth. There are leaves and earth mounded at the mouth of the hole, but once we had walked down into the hole, the roof rose above us and it was not claustrophobic. Bats hung upside down at the far end.

The cannons installed in 1796, at the time the last fortress was constructed, also have survived, though the wooden carriages they once rested on have long since rotted away, and the long iron forms now rest on weedy grass. Because this was an English fortress, some of the cannons bear the curling cipher of King George III, the intermittently mad king fought by the colonies during the American Revolution. Most of these cannons face the downriver side of the island, from which foreign attacks as well as friendly traders came. The king's beautiful monogram is topped with a crown. This is the same monarch who saw Caribbean planters become richer than kings, and is said to have remarked when he saw a Jamaican planter's extravagant carriage in Weymouth, "Sugar, sugar, eh? All *that* sugar!"

In Freetown a week later, I met an angry woman named Sia Fayia. Fayia owned a street-corner restaurant redolent of spices. The restaurant was dark and cool, and one of its walls was painted with murals, most of which she was having painted over. The mural of a young, slender Queen Elizabeth II and a bored-looking Prince Philip were about to be whitewashed and replaced with a painting of the *Amistad* captives, Sierra Leoneans aboard a Cuban slave ship who revolted against their captivity and whose trials began in a Connecticut court in 1839. The only mural that was going to remain showed a terrified black man hanging from a rope over a rushing river. In the river below him, a crocodile spread wide its bloody jaws, while on the shore a roaring lion waited. A rat gnawed busily at the unraveling rope to which the man clung, screaming.

The next mural would show "Bonce Island," Sia Fayia said, "the nightmare." Stern-faced and stout, she shook a DVD of Steven Spielberg's *Amistad* in my face, saying fiercely, "How do you escape from the nightmare? How? How?"

And then she answered her question: "Only by awakening."

And by remembering, I thought, when I was back on the island a few days later. More and more, I was coming to understand that the logbooks had led me into one of world history's most terrible stories, and then led me to that story's ground, its *earth*. Dudley Saltonstall's sea voyages, recounted so calmly, do not show the screaming man clinging to the unraveling rope, nor do they show John Easton's beautiful house and its treasures; but those, too, are part of the story. These are the extremes the history of slavery encompasses.

The unanswerable question, of course, is whose nightmare did Mrs. Fayia refer to? The continuing injustice that governs the lives of millions of black Americans is not a nightmare for many white Americans, for whom a two-tiered society with black people at the bottom is not a problem at all, or even worth contemplating. Even when perfectly articulated, as it has been in many books and movies and art forms, the story of Americans of African descent doesn't *stay* told.

Modern website developers use the word *sticky* to denote site characteristics that keep users coming back, and that help keep the site in view, in use, and valuable. Using that term, the story of African American people has not proven particularly sticky for white society, and it means that the story itself must be told over and over, from the beginning. It has not yet been absorbed into the family of stories told and retold about America.

I often feel that New England historians are impatient and heartily sick of me. I don't blame them. "Anne, people already *know* this," a historian said to me in 2007. Many of these historians, perhaps most of them, are already deeply familiar with the story that is still new to me and that I want to share. They know the names and the dates and the awful numbers, and they have written about them. What am I *on* about? And yet, my only defense is that the story of injustice and suffering they know, and have documented, still has not made its way into the national narrative. What the historians know has not become truly public, and until it does, I can be of use.

THE STORY OF A STONE

From that moment five months earlier when I had first shown Joseph Opala the pages of the logbooks, he had insisted that I needed to visit Bence Island, and that seeing the island would help me understand the trauma it embodies and symbolizes, despite its tiny size. My brother and sister were fearful for my safety because of the social disruption and poverty that followed a ghastly and just-ended decade of civil war in Sierra Leone, but I knew that if I did not go, I would always feel like a coward, and that I had failed my story. Joe said that Bence Island is the slavery trade's insect frozen in amber, and I simply could not resist the powerful draw of its history.

Bence Island is about 350 feet wide, and only 1,600 feet long. We walked easily from one end of the island to the other. Open to the sky, the ruins are located on a small rise so that whenever we turned to look back, they seemed to be right behind us. The slaves held for sale at Bence Island had been brought from 600 miles north and south of the island, and from as far inland as 100 miles. Some would have been brought in rough dugout canoes to the shallow upriver side of the island, a short cross-island walk from the jetty where we had landed. Many of the people brought for sale at Bence Island were skilled in the agriculture of growing rice, and came from cultures that had been growing rice for centuries.

Scholars Judith Carney, Peter Wood, Joseph Opala, and others have described what happened here as a kind of technology transfer: when colonial South Carolina and Georgia began growing rice in the first half of the eighteenth century, these African rice growers were the slaves of choice because they brought not only their labor, but their skills at growing rice in a tidewater cultivation system that had originated centuries earlier. When Richard Oswald's partner Henry Laurens advertised his cargoes of "Prime Windward Slaves" in Charleston's newspapers, he was communicating that these people

By the time traveler John Corry visited "Bance" Island in 1805, the international slave trade had an infernal reputation and was soon to be made illegal. Visitors like Corry and others suggested that Sierra Leone was a natural center for agriculture, though after the English stepped aside from the slave trade in 1808, the island was the site of a sawmill for several decades. From *Observations Upon the Windward Coast of Africa* by Joseph Corry

were rice growers. They knew how to "transform tidal swamps into productive rice fields."

Ricing, the word that had baffled me when I had seen it months earlier in Saltonstall's logbooks, meant bringing barrels of rice on board the ship, where it would be the primary food of the captives on their way to the New World. They ate it with a peppery sauce.

In the center of the island was once a village populated by the grommetos. There are many variations on the word *grommeto*, which is Portuguese in origin, but grommetos lived all along the West African coast and were involved in the slaving trade in many capacities. For Bence Island's grommetos, participating in the trade meant that they were protected from being sold into slavery, and so were their families. At the height of the island's prosperity in the 1750s and 1760s, as many as 100 grommetos lived on the island. Their chief lived with them, and they had a graveyard separate from that of the white work-ers. The grommetos were a world within a world, and their thatched-roofed huts appear on old drawings of the island.

Like other Englishmen of his time, visitor Joseph Corry believed that proximity to white people was good for Africans. In his book of observations on the Windward Coast, he noted that the grommetos on Bence Island were artisan-level carpenters, joiners, masons, and iron-smiths, and "would deserve the approbation even of the connoisseur in these arts." With a kind of condescension that he couldn't have recog-nized, he added, "In many other instances they discover a genius of the most intelligent character, and a decency in their dress and manners distinguished from that among the surrounding tribes; which is the never failing consequence of the influence of the arts of civilized soci-ety over barbarous customs and habits."

Anna Maria Falconbridge visited the grommetos' village, called Adam's Town, and commented that their homes were "quite clean and neat," and that the residents greeted her respectfully.

Anna Maria was younger than her volatile husband, abolitionist Al-exander Falconbridge, and she did not share his deep hatred of the slave trade. In her narrative, she was frank about her disgust with his drinking and his temper, and it seems that her feeling for him died before he did. A few weeks after his death, she married a man who was connected to the slave trade and left Sierra Leone forever. But she seems to have enjoyed her visits to Bence Island and found the antislavery endeavor that had brought her and her husband to Sierra Leone ill advised. (A group of English abolitionists were attempting to establish a settlement in Sierra Leone for freed slaves from the Ca-ribbean and the Americas. The history of the early settlement, called Granville Town for abolitionist Granville Sharp, was fraught with dis-ease, miscommunication, and conflicts with the locals.)

After waving her husband off to a day of dealing with whites and African traders who were, not unreasonably for that time and place, skeptical about the concept of a permanently free black population in a locale where the slave trade had flourished for two centuries, Anna Maria would settle in for a day of socializing with company agents and traders at the fortress. She also took guided tours around the island, and included in her narrative novelistically precise vignettes of the Africans she met. She didn't mention in her narrative the two-hole "Goff" course that naturalist Henry Smeathman saw when he was on the island in 1773, and which he described as "a very pretty exercise for a warm climate as there is nothing violent in it except the single blow."

On one of her island walks, Anna Maria visited the graveyard of white men who had died on the island, and she noted that the quiet grove was shaded by orange trees. On my last visit to the island, we went there, too. There are no longer orange trees around the graveyard, but the area had been cleared for us, and I saw the grave of a Danish sea captain, as well as that of a slave trader named William Cleavland. Saltonstall mentioned in his logbook that Captain Cleavland sailed past the *Africa* on March 29, 1757, in a schooner with thirty slaves on board, and that the two ships hailed each other. A successful and widely known trader, Cleavland owned substantial properties in the West Indies, and when he died in 1758 on Bence Island, he left a fortune to his mulatto daughters, one of whom is said to have bought a plantation in South Carolina.

Seeing Cleavland's grave, and remembering the logbook entry that mentioned him, made a stone drop in my heart. A piece of eighteenth-century paper archived in Hartford, Connecticut, had led me to a grave on an abandoned island in West Africa. This was the connection I wanted to make: to let the past speak *through* me, and to be its instrument.

Using sheets of handmade paper and graphite that I had brought from home, I tried to trace the words from the grave of Thomas Knight, an Englishman who had supervised slave trading on Bence for eighteen years. Anna Maria Falconbridge saw the same grave on her visit in 1791. Knight had shipped cargoes of slaves to planter Henry Laurens, the Charleston merchant who was a kingpin in the American slave trade and followed John Hancock as president of the Continental Congress. (Through the influence of his own son John, who believed the colonists were wrong to demand freedom of the English while practicing slavery themselves, Laurens said he hated slavery, but that it was a system forced on the colonies by the British.)

All of the headstones were rough, tilting, and in poor condition. In the heat of midday, the stick of graphite was melting onto my hands before I could rub it cleanly against the paper, and I couldn't get a clear image of the lettering on the stone. I finally gave up and, pulling the rice paper away from Knight's grave, saw that only one word was even faintly legible:

Memory.

THE SLAUGHTERHOUSE

*Some wet blowing weather having occasioned
the portholes to be shut and the grating to be covered,
fluxes and fevers among the negroes ensued.*

ALEXANDER FALCONBRIDGE

Amoebic dysentery was the leading cause of death among captives during the Middle Passage, and one of the most feared diseases of the seventeenth and eighteenth centuries. Dudley Saltonstall and others of his era called it the "bloody flux," though they did not know that it was an intestinal infection caused by a parasitic microorganism that contaminated water and food. The medium of transmission was human feces and fecal bacteria. For captives who were often marched for days on their way to the coast, held in barracoons and enclosures littered with human waste, and fed dirty food and contaminated water, and whose longevity needed to last only until they were off their traders' hands, the disease was ever present.

On April 17, 1757, the *Good Hope* left Bence Island and sailed down to the mouth of the Sierra Leone River and Frenchman's Bay before heading a few days north toward the Isles de Los. In his usual phonetic style of spelling, Saltonstall called them the "Edless," or "Edlesses," his approximation of the Portuguese name for this archipelago of slaving islands: Las Idolas, or the Islands of Idols. He noted a week later, on April 24, that some of the slaves were "not very well."

Amoebic dysentery has an incubation period that ranges from fifteen days to three months, so the captives Saltonstall described as "not very well" might have been infected weeks earlier during the captivity that preceded their sale at Bence Island or another outpost, if Alexander Urqhart had purchased them before arriving at Bence.

The week before the men sailed, Saltonstall noted in his logbook that he had heard from a Rhode Island slave ship captain that Captain

Alexander Dondass, who was headed from the coast of Africa to the West Indies "with 150 Prime Slaves on Board," had been "cut of[f]" and he and his crew murdered. The only ones who had been spared were the carpenter—an essential crew member—and the cabin boy, who was probably just a child.

Saltonstall wrote that the vessel had been run ashore, but he didn't say where, or who had attacked the ship. The "prime slaves" could have risen against their captors, which was a frequent occurrence, or Captain Dondass might have cheated or in some way angered a powerful black trader or chief. He might have "panyar'd" an African trader, that is, bought the trader's captives and then grabbed the trader too. Because a panyar was considered a particularly egregious betrayal of trade and always brought reprisals, even if the white perpetrator got away with the deed, black traders would punish the next ship they saw. Dondass might simply have been in the wrong place at the wrong time.

In 1734, English captain William Snelgrave described "the natives" freely bringing on board various commodities for trade, including "Negroes and Elephants Teeth," except when a panyar had occurred:

> Which, to the great scandal of both the *English* and the *French*, has too often been done, namely by their forcibly carrying away the Traders under some slight pretense of having received an Injury from them. And this has put a stop to the Trade of the particular place where it has happened for a long time; and innocent People, who have come here to trade in small Vessels, have suffered for their Countrymens Villainy: Several in my time have been surprised by the Natives, and the People destroyed out of revenge.

News traveled fast on the coast, because the trade at this period was so intense and there were lots of ships from Europe and the colonies. These men were in competition with one another, and yet in some ways, they were all in it together. They were always eager, Joe Opala told me, for news of wars, uprisings, and trouble spots on the long African coast, because their lives depended on such information.

Engaged in a trade that later would be condemned, they were also leveraging a global system of commerce that rested on two hemispheres and had the potential to make them rich. It paid to look sharp and to stay informed.

As they moved away from the African coast, however, Saltonstall and Urqhart had a more immediate problem than the fate of Dondass and his men. The malaise that had affected several of the captives had progressed to wracking abdominal cramps and bowel movements filled with blood.

Though he chronicled their decline in a telegraphic way—from "not very well" to "died this day"—Saltonstall was learning very early in his career about a ferocious and often fatal disease. Those afflicted could have as many as twenty bowel movements in twenty-four hours, sometimes suffering for several days before dying. Physicians at the time believed that the bloody flux came from stagnant or swampy air, or from various "humours." Daniel Defoe thought it might be caused by eating too much fruit.

Before he became an abolitionist, Alexander Falconbridge, husband of the lively Anna Maria, was an English surgeon who served on slaving voyages to the coast of Africa during the 1780s. Falconbridge later provided powerful testimony to the British Parliament about the slave trade, particularly regarding the suffering of the captives and the hideous physical abuse of the ordinary seamen aboard the slave ships.

Falconbridge was also impolitic, had trouble organizing his thoughts, was a severe alcoholic, and was so zealous in his attacks on slavery that some abolitionists feared he might do more harm than good. At the time of his testimony, he was barely thirty, and two years later, on the coast of Sierra Leone, he died of his drinking on the same day that he was fired by the antislavery group that had sent him to Africa.

opposite:

On May 5, 1757, a day of fresh breezes and clear weather, Dudley Saltonstall noted in his logbook, "this 24 hours Died 3 Small Slaves with the Flux." Logbooks, Courtesy of the Connecticut State Library

6.thDay	H	K	Fk	Course	Winds	Remarks
	2	2	1	SW	WNW	Teusday May 3.^d 1757
	4	7	·			Fresh Breese & Cloudy
	6	3	1			
	8	4	·	SWBW	NWBW	Slaves Groing Better
	10	4	·			
	12	3	·			
	2	3	·			S.K^d
	4	3	·			
	6	2	1	N.^o	WNW	
	8	2	1	NBW		
	10	2	·	NNW		S.K^d
	12	2	m	WBS	NWNW	Latt.^d ⊙ Obs.ⁿ 9:50 N.^o
		71				

Course	Distance	D.Lat.^e	Dep:ⁿ	Lat.^d Acc.	D.Long.^e	Long.^d in	Mer.ⁿ Dist
S:40.W.^t	45 M	0:35 S.	0.29 W	9:53	6:30 L.^t	17:17 ^t	WBS M. W

	H	K	Fk	Course	Winds	Remarks
	2	3	·	WSW	NW	Wednesday May 4.th 1757
	4	3	1			Fresh Breise & Hazey
	6	3	·			
	8	3	·	WBS	NWBN	1 Man Slave Dangerously
	10	3	·			ill
	12	3	·			
	2	2	1			at 4 AM a Man Slave Died
	4	3	·			Fresh Breese & Hazey
	6	4	·	WNW	N.^o	
	8	4	·	WBN		
	10	4	1			Latt.^d ⊙ Observation 9:37 N.^o
	12	5	·			
		73	74			

W.S.S.^o	79 Mile	0:12 S.	1:18 W	9:38 N	1:19 W	18:36	301 M W.^t

	H	K	Fk	Course	Winds	Remarks
	2	5	·	WBN	NBW	Thirsday May 5.th 1757
	4	5	·			Fresh Breese & Clear
	6	5	·			
	8	4	·			this 24 hours Died 3 Small Slaves
	10	4	·			with the Flux —— 165 Slaves
	12	4	·			Remains Living on Board
	2	3	1			Fresh Breese
	4	4	·			
	6	5	·			
	8	5	·			
	10	4	1			Latt.^d ⊙ Obs. 9:35 N.^o
	12	4	m			
		107				

W.^t 107	Distance	0:0	1:47 W	9:37 N.^o	1:48 W	20:24	403. M W.^t

But he knew what he had seen and experienced aboard the *Tarter*, the *Emilia*, and the *Alexander*, and his experience supported what has become the most famous image of the slave trade itself: the diagram of the British merchant slave ship called the *Brookes*. The 297-ton *Brookes* was, after the Regulated Slave Trade, Act of 1788 (also called the Dolben Act), allowed to carry approximately 430 slaves. Named for the antislavery member of Parliament who had sponsored it, and intended to be a humane measure, the Dolben Act specified that five slaves could be carried for every 3 tons of the ship's carrying capacity up to 201 tons, and then one slave for every ton over that.

But Falconbridge had witnessed the way slave ships frequently circumvented that law by such close stowing of the captives that they lay interlocked, without even the claustrophobic amount of space allowed by the Dolben Act. The *Brookes* had on at least three voyages carried more than 600 slaves to the New World, and on a voyage shortly before it became Exhibit A among abolitionists, it had carried 740. Given these conditions, it is not surprising that amoebic dysentery was the ghastly—though initially invisible—boarder on slave ships. Historians Daniel Mannix and Malcolm Cowley have described the Middle Passage as "a crossroad and marketplace of diseases," and the place where the smallpox, measles, and venereal diseases of Europe met the lethal fevers of Africa.

The *Good Hope* was a sloop, a smaller style of vessel often seen in the slaving trade at this time, and usually ranging from 20 to 50 tons. The Dolben Act was still thirty years in the future, but by its regulations the *Good Hope*'s cargo should have been not more than about 80 captives, even if the vessel were 50 tons or a little larger. Saltonstall noted that the cargo was 169 slaves on board when the sloop left the coast, well above the maximum number that practice and concern for the captives' health would have dictated. The Dolben Act also sought to make mandatory the presence of an experienced ship's physician on every slaving voyage, and to award a bonus to commanders and ships' crews who landed their human cargoes with a fatality rate of not more than 3 percent.

But I was learning that although the slave trade itself was a complicated business—and one that demanded nautical skill, financial acumen, a constant accommodation of violence and suffering, as well as a steady supply, on the African side, of black human beings—the bottom line was simple: the more slaves landed alive and well in the Caribbean and the Americas, the more money made. Stowing the captives closely together held the potential for greater profits, though it made this part of their captivity one of even greater suffering. Scholar Marcus Rediker has suggested that a slave ship was, in and of itself, an instrument of torture.

The captives were held in the heat and darkness, lying with headroom on rough bare planks in a pitching ship, packed closely together with their fellows, some of whom were seasick—which was epidemic at the beginning of the voyage—and some of whom were excreting blood and feces. Three decades later, Englishman Alexander Falconbridge used the word "slaughterhouse" to describe the situation that confronted Saltonstall in May of 1757; and he later wrote that the stench below decks during an outbreak of flux on one of his ships was so terrible that he collapsed and had to be physically carried back up onto the deck.

"Your captains and mates . . . must neither have dainty fingers nor dainty noses," wrote the commander of the Royal African Company at Cape Coast Castle in 1690.

English naturalist and entomologist Henry Smeathman, who explored Sierra Leone in the 1770s and lived on its coastal islands for four years, described the horror of a slave ship in the Sierra Leone River with sick on board. "Alas! What a scene of misery and distress is a full slaved ship in the rains. The clanking of chains, the groans of the sick and the stench of the whole. . . . Two or three slaves thrown overboard every day dying of fever flux, measles, worms all together. All the day the chains rattling."

Five days after beginning the Atlantic crossing to the Caribbean, Saltonstall noted again, cryptically, "Slaves Not Very Well." Two days

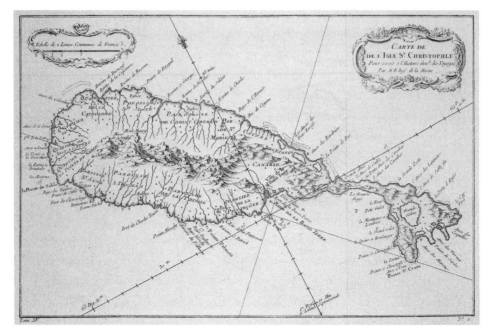

Scholar Richard Dunn says that the Caribbean island of St. Christopher, or St. Kitts as it is now more often called, began cultivating sugar in the first half of the seventeenth century. By the middle of the eighteenth century, when the Connecticut traders in the logbooks visited, the island was a frequent port of call for colonial and English ships. From the author's collection

later, a man died. A day after that, three children. "This 24 Hours Died 2 Small Boy Slaves of the Flux," Saltonstall wrote on May 17. In the first twenty days of the passage from Sierra Leone, twelve captives died; ten of them were children. The gender of three of the children, all of whom died on the eighth day of the voyage, was not given. They were described, simply, as "small slaves."

Anything that would have eased their suffering—family, the sounds of home, even fresh air—would have been denied to them. The adults, both men, probably died of heart failure, exhaustion, dehydration, or a perforated bowel. The violent contractions of the dysentery some-times tore the bowels in two. The children died of dehydration and exhaustion. Thirty years later, a French slave dealer in Bordeaux found that ample portions of clean food and water helped combat the flux, but at midcentury, Saltonstall would have had neither viable medicines nor any idea how to cure the sufferers or prevent the spread of the disease. Neither the children—who were particularly susceptible to dehydration—nor the adults would have been given the large amounts of fresh water and food they needed. The prevailing remedy then was to starve the sufferer.

The below-decks spaces where the captives were held were furnished with "necessary tubs," which were conically shaped latrines, but the virulence of the dysentery and the way the people were so closely packed together often made it impossible for the sick to reach the tubs. They would have suffered thirst and stabbing pains in the stomach. They would have been in too much pain to sleep, and as they lay in their own blood and excrement, they would have been conscious of their misery because delirium did not occur until the very end.

The *Good Hope* reached the island of St. Kitts with 151 slaves. Two more adults and four more children had died, bringing the total loss of life to eighteen, or about 11 percent of the original cargo. This was a standard figure for the time, although casualties on transatlantic voyages were sometimes much higher. There is no way to know how many of the survivors were infected or about to manifest symptoms of the disease when they were put ashore on St. Kitts and sold into permanent bondage. Amoebic dysentery was the leading cause of death among slaves newly arrived in the Caribbean, but by then, a dysentery-stricken captive was a problem for the purchaser, and not the shipper.

Saltonstall did not offer commentary on the outbreak or on what must have been scenes from a nightmare.

At St. Kitts, Saltonstall consulted a Dr. Balderson about his jaw, which he thought he might have dislocated on board the *Africa* weeks earlier. The doctor said the jawbone was too stiff to be reset, and gave him an ointment to relax it.

… Imployd abo Rigging Carp. & Joiner making awning
… Making a Pump Can   No Trade at all

…rday July 15th 1758 this 24 hours Light Winds & pleas. W..
… Imployd overhawling Blocks Carp. & Joiner Making
…g — No Trade only Bought Some Corn & plantins

…ay July 16th this 24 hours Light Winds & pleas. Wea. People
…yd abo. Jobs Carp. & Joiner abo. the awning the Cap. on
… Wanton — ~~No too~~ Purchased one boy Slave of Quaquom

…day July 17. this 24 hours Light Winds & pleas. Wea. Peo,
…oyd over hawling tobacco Carp. & Joiner abo. the awning
…ade at all — Saild for Sirrenam the Large Dutch S.
…500 & od Slaves onboard

…ay July 18. this 24 hours Light Winds & pleas. Wea. Peop
…y in ye Hold & fetching Brazeal Tobacco from a Dute…
…Cap. Buley — Purchased one man Slave

…esday July 19. this 24 hours Light Winds but a Large …
…le Imployd picking Tobacco No Trade at all

…day July 20. this 24 hours Calm & little Wind People Imploy…
…Hold Cooper a Cutting Rum Hd Purchased ~~all~~ Two Slave…
…ssels in ye Rhode Except Three Poor Rum Men
…d the yaul up to clean   broacht a bl Bee…

…y July 20 this 24 hours Calm Weather People Imployd ove…
…ld & found a Hogs. No. 86 Leaked all out No. 85 only 54 Gal. in …
…gin to ye Cap. — Leakage ocationed by all ye Head Hoops fly…
…rade this 24 hours — the agreed with my Lord to Send a man
…to accraw after ye Longboat for 4 Gal. Trade Rum

…rday July 21. this 24 hours Calm Wea. People Imployd fi…
…heads with Water & with Rum Cooper a Cutting Hogs…
…d from ye Longboat by a Letter from… Understood …
…g at Mumford with 3 Slaves on board

…day July 22. this 24 hours Calm & hazey Weather at 10
… Ship to W. Ward which we Suppos'd to be the English Man of …

THREE

Trouble in Mind

A BOOK WITH MANY BOOKMARKS

Belief and seeing are often both wrong.
ROBERT MCNAMARA

On the day my mother was diagnosed with dementia, the specialist said, "Now she can never be alone." My brother Chas and sister Kate had taken Mama to a geriatric psychiatrist to be evaluated for her memory problems, problems we thought might be related to depression or exhaustion from having cared for our father for almost a decade.

She was living with me then because her loneliness after Dad's death was so acute. My brother and sister and I thought she should be with one of us. Of the three of us, I had the most room and the fewest responsibilities.

I had hired a woman of about Mama's age to come in and spend the days with her. They would go for walks, and take drives for coffee, and clean my house. My mother had always loved to read, and we had often shared books, but she couldn't seem to concentrate anymore. I noticed that the Jan Karon novel she had brought with her was bristling with bookmarks, as if she couldn't remember where she had left off. But my house was spotless.

I told Mama that we had arranged for her to talk to a doctor about how she was feeling, and that Chas and Kate would be with her at the appointment. "I'm looking forward to getting some tips on how to re-member things," Mama said. "I don't want to turn into a forgetful old lady."

When I got home from work that spring day, my brother and sister were there with Mama. She looked crestfallen, and asked if she could put on her bathrobe. Kate met me in the kitchen as I was taking off my coat, and just shook her head. I remember the lemony April light in my living room, and that we all sat there, feeling that something big had happened to our family. Dad had been dead for not quite six months, and now, what we knew in our hearts, and had known for months, had a name.

"Mum, the doctor says you can't live alone," my brother said. Chas was retiring that spring from thirty years of teaching middle- and high-school English. He has a calm, musical voice, and after years at the head of a classroom, he's used to repeating things. "Your memory isn't strong enough for you to manage by yourself, so we need to make a plan." He didn't say *dementia*.

Mama had already forgotten the memory tests of earlier that after-noon, but seemed to understand that something had led to her children being in a room together, looking solemn. "How 'bout I go back home, and check in with you every day?" she suggested.

"Tried that," Chas said simply. Because her short-term memory was gone, Mama couldn't remember whether she had eaten, made a phone call, taken her medication, or done any other daily task. When she had been alone in the house where we had grown up, it was not unusual for her to call many times in an evening, though her manners were so good that she would ask, "Did I already call you tonight?"

I remembered the microwave oven and the baked potato.

Right after Dad died, Mama wasn't eating well, so Chas bought a microwave oven for her to cook baked potatoes, her favorite food. He knew she would regard heating her large oven for a single potato as wasteful. On the microwave oven, he had taped a brief list of instruc-tions that she could follow to cook the potato.

When I dropped by to see her after work one day, I noticed that she had written above my brother's instructions: "Put food in first." I learned in the next months that dementia is not just a single kind of forgetting, and it's not the same for every person who has it. The disease is as individual as the sufferer, and has an odd way of encompassing fragments of information from the past and the present; but it is profound, and erases logic as well as memory because without a stable past, anything might be possible. (At a later point, Mama thought she was being held prisoner in the dungeon of a school for boys and called 911 to tell the police.)

With promises that we would meet and talk again, my family left, and I made my mother a bowl of soup. It was a turkey leek soup from Julia Child that I had made on the weekend, with Mama's help. She didn't say much at dinner, though I was getting used to her silences. She couldn't manage the call and response of real conversation anymore, though at this point, she still seemed to be listening, and she liked to be read to.

She wanted to go to bed early, and there was still a little daylight left as I sat on the edge of the guest bed and held her hand. I saw that she had worn her robe and slippers to bed. "I'm sorry, Mama," I said. "You lose Dad and now this."

"It seems like kind of a dirty trick," she whispered.

I put the hall light on for her, and left her door cracked open so that she could see the light. I remembered that she had done the same thing for my sister and me, when we were small.

Downstairs, I sat with a book in my lap and wondered how I could have been so blind. I knew that Mama's memory was increasingly bad, and that she couldn't remember how she spent her days with the companion. Though she had always managed the family finances and investments, she couldn't balance her checkbook anymore. She hid her medications and insisted she had run out. She wanted to put on the same dress every day and couldn't remember the name of the newspaper where I had worked for years. At odd moments, but more and more often, she was terrified. After we'd bought groceries together one day, she asked me, in a panic, how I remembered where I'd parked my car.

I was on deadline one day when a neighbor called my office to say that there was a fire truck, sirens blaring and lights flashing, in front of my house and that she was heading over. It had been a day of heavy rain, and Mama didn't recognize the sound of the sump pump when it clanked to life in the basement. Frightened by the loud *clunk* of the pump as it pushed the water out of the house, she and her caretaker had decided to call the fire department. By the time I got home, the fire truck had returned to the station, and she remembered nothing of the afternoon's excitement.

The previous Thanksgiving, Mama had suffered endlessly over how to make a pumpkin pie. During the fifty-five years of her married life, she'd made hundreds of pies, but suddenly, she couldn't remember how to put one together. My solution was to buy enough ingredients for several pumpkin pies, so that if she wasn't happy with the first one, we could make more. I told her not to worry, and that we would make a great pie together.

But I was missing the point. And two nights before Thanksgiving, I found her in the kitchen a little before dawn, running her hands around the edges of her old Pyrex pie plate. "I'm reviewing," she said.

I had had so many plans for my mother. She was a decade younger than my father, and he had been ill for most of his eighties. She was seventy-eight and still so beautiful that people turned to look at her in the street. We knew she would survive Dad, and we had a wonderful widowhood all planned for her. My sister and I had picked out a garden apartment for her in the same neighborhood as our family home, we were going to take crafts classes with her, and we even had a kind and wealthy widower, a longtime family friend, selected. She just needed to recover from Dad's death, get her appetite back, and rejoin the world.

That was all.

A PLATFORM FOR MEMORY

The art of remembering, William James said, is the art of thinking. A philosopher and physician, James discovered that to help the students in his physiology classes at Harvard remember a new idea, or to remember something new himself, he needed to connect the new idea to a piece of information already held. "The connecting *is* the thinking," he said, "and if we attend clearly to the connection, the connected thing will certainly be likely to remain within recall."

The father of American psychology, James devoted long and passionate study to the formation of human memory. He saw human beings as the sum of what they knew and remembered. He believed that we receive information viscerally, but that our later recall of that information is both physical and psychological.

His brother, novelist Henry James, explored the terrain of memory in his fiction, and although William lived a century before the advent of magnetic resonance imaging and the hard science of how human beings remember, modern neuroscience supports much of what he said more than a century ago: for new information to be remembered, it needs a structure on which to rest. It needs a context.

I began to think of memory as a kind of platform, one to which lengths of wood can be added to make it larger. A good platform is a stable structure with many separate boards combining to make a whole, and a well-made platform can support objects of varying weight and significance while it makes room for them. The objects on the platform may differ in size, but they are in full view of each other. A newly constructed platform for Connecticut's relationship with slavery would provide room for the logbooks, for the captured human beings transported from Africa to the Caribbean and the colonies, for the beautiful possessions once owned by John Easton, for the 1758 newspaper account of the disastrous last voyage in the logbooks, and for the handful of glass beads I brought back from the jetty on Bence Island.

This stable platform would show the links between objects that might seem disparate, but which are, in deepest fact, connected by the history they touched.

American slavery was never a story that was just about black people and their white owners in the South, but a story that links Americans everywhere to each other and to the past. Our lack of a stable platform, or view, of the past helps keep the damage of slavery alive because when trauma is denied, the suffering of its descendants becomes worse.

My mother's memory platform had lost objects that varied in size and importance. Her marriage, her children, her life skills as a homemaker and secretary all tumbled from the platform, and the disparity between the truths she had once known about herself and the utter loss of those truths made her unable to function with independence and clarity. The loss of her memory was so profound that she became helpless. (Our love protected her from degradation, and the money she and Dad had saved made her life as good as it could be, but her fate, after a life of tender service to her family and neighbors, was a terrible one.)

In helping to care for her, I saw connections to my country's history. From America's memory platform, many realities also have fallen. The national narrative about how the country was founded, then prospered and moved forward does not give slavery the major place it actually held.

Slavery was not the "sad chapter" in an otherwise glorious trajectory. Slavery was not a chapter but the book itself, and our nation's form of hereditary bondage was the cornerstone of our making, our creation. That crucial history fell from the memory platform, but what did *not* fall was the racial prejudice that preceded and enabled slavery and that was deepened and enlarged by slavery itself. This racial prejudice was essential if a population so palpably human was to be held down; and its great power can still be felt today, unchanged by a generation of books, movies, college courses, and social training designed to correct the historical record and conquer hatred. The problem is not a lack of accurate material, but one of recognition.

What if we could regain the story we lost and that we need so much? This question, which is at the marrow of my life, is a generative one. I am trying, with the story of my mother and those long-ago ships, to sift and reconcile, to get something back, and to bring a long misunderstood past back into the light, where it can help us and, as Sia Fayia said to me in Africa, awaken us from the continuing nightmare of our own history.

If a context had been created for the system of enslavement that dominated and shaped America's first two centuries, and if white culture had, right from the very beginning, acknowledged the key nature of slavery as a cruel and fabulously successful economic engine, I believe that the America we occupy today would be different. Black Americans would not trail whites in nearly every standard by which we measure the good life, and we could try to understand what happened between 1660 and 1860. We could begin to see why racial prejudice still governs our landscape and places limitations on the lives of many black Americans.

But the story of America's hundreds of thousands of enslaved people—and by 1860 there were 4 million slaves here—is a story to break the heart and from which national memory instinctively torques away. In its totality, the reality that their lives and labor were worth more than all the nation's railroads and factories defies imagining, so, by and large, white Americans have not imagined it. It defies understanding as well, so we have tried to move past it without looking it squarely in the face. We don't know how damaging slavery was because we don't know our own history in the ways that we need to, in the ways that could help us address our present, still-unequal society. This is a book about white agency, but we are all the survivors and in the slipstream of the history that was lived here. White people will find their own past and black people will find verification and validation for their suffering if we are willing to take on this shared history. If we can explore and integrate an alternate and truer view of the past, the future will look different too.

Americans love "consensus" history—that shared story of how our pioneer spirit and a group of exceptional men helped us break away from an ancient European country and become not just a handful of loosely organized and very disparate colonies, but a nation. Much of that narrative is true, but it is a narrative with a secret at its heart. And it is a secret that makes us look worse than even bad old Great Britain, which led the international slave trade but did not have enslavement on its home territory.

By the time eighteen-year-old Dudley Saltonstall clambered up the gangway to the *Africa* in 1757, colonial America was a society that held slaves. These captive people were held not just in the South, but in the mid-Atlantic and in New York, New Jersey, New Hampshire, Massachusetts, Connecticut, and Rhode Island. By 1760 there were an estimated 400,000 enslaved people in the colonies, and after the introduction of the cotton gin—Eli Whitney's wonderfully simple engine for separating the cotton wool from its seeds—that number grew larger.

But those people we held were living beings, utterly human, and to hold them in bondage required white people, I believe, to deny their humanity. Captives could not be people who loved and grieved, who had dreams beyond being servants to white people. Oppression requires dehumanization, because we don't want to feel badly about ourselves.

In the South, the great-great-grandsons of Civil War soldiers told me about the gentle treatment plantation owners showed their slaves, and said that yes, some planters were cruel, but most were not. In the North, I was questioned constantly about the Underground Railroad, which shepherded freedom-seeking captives to Ohio, Canada, and other cities in the North.

"Are you going to tell both sides of the story?" a woman in an adult education class in New Jersey asked me in a hostile tone.

But the historical problem for anyone who would make sense of our divided country is that American enslavement is not a story with equivalencies. The Underground Railroad, which is believed to have helped 100,000 captive people escape to freedom, is not equal to the other half of the millions of black people held in captivity between the mid-seventeenth century and the mid-nineteenth. Those 100,000 do not balance the scale with captive millions on the other side.

An adequate and well-made memory platform for two centuries of human bondage would include those oppressed millions, the killing nature of their captivity, America's financial dependence on and addiction to enslaved labor, and a system of racial discrimination that is, even a decade into the twenty-first century, still immensely powerful.

Eighty years before William James stood in those Harvard classrooms in the 1870s, lawyer and journalist Theodore Dwight gave a speech in Hartford to the Connecticut Society for the Promotion of Freedom and Relief of Persons Unlawfully Holden in Bondage. Passionately antislavery in his outlook, Dwight said to his audience that although slavery should be ended and was a condition that "embitters every enjoyment," slavery in Connecticut was "essentially different." Slaves in the state—and there were then about 2,000—were not harshly treated, he said, but "indulged in many amusements" and "flourishing and happy." One can hear the echo of Bontemps's black "invisibility" scholarship here, because black captives in Connecticut had already begun, at the time of Dwight's speech in 1794, to petition for their freedom. And as the narratives of former nineteenth-century slaves Frederick Douglass, James Mars, Sojourner Truth, William Grimes, and others attest, there was no such thing as a good enslavement.

In his blissfully inconsistent remarks, Dwight was doing several very human things, all of them damaging to the truth. A distinguished and fair-minded man, Dwight was helping to build a mythology that endures to this day: slavery in the North was a relatively benign institution, more like an indenture, only without an end date. This intellectual and emotional framework, which probably allowed Dwight to find slaveholding among people he knew bearable, also helped the history makers who followed him recast human bondage—at least New England's form of human bondage—in a kinder, gentler light. Southern writers and historians have tried to do the same thing with stories of benevolent owners, intact enslaved families, and slaves refusing to leave the plantations even when they could.

Dwight and those who shared his views distorted the record in their own day and for the day that had preceded them, as well as the one that would follow.

In her history of New London published in 1852, Frances Manwaring Caulkins wrote that it was her ardent desire "to engage the present generation in this ennobling study of their past history, and to awaken a sentiment of deeper and more affectionate sympathy with our ancestors, than has hitherto been felt."

A descendant of the port city's early settlers, Caulkins included "people" stories in her nearly 700-page narrative, and told the stories of women's achievements, which was not common in histories of the mid-nineteenth century. But as exhaustively researched as her history is—and it is a gold mine of detailed scholarship—she left out key pieces of the New London story. Slave ships and slave ship captains are not identified as such in Caulkins's history, though Saltonstall appears in his role as a naval commander. New London's slaves are a shadowy population, barely mentioned. Captive people appear being handed down to family members, and in 1739 as a group of "ten negro slaves taken to prison for being out unreasonably in a frolic at old Wright's." Three who had gone to the party without permission were whipped; the seven who "had leave" were dismissed with a fine, Caulkins noted carefully.

Nearly halfway through her narrative, and describing events in 1714, Caulkins wrote, "At this period, many families in town owned slaves, for domestic service; some but one; others two or three; very few more than four."

A committed abolitionist, Caulkins put her energies to work for the antislavery cause, and though she wrote at length about the native American populations before, during, and after the settlement of New London, New London's captive population scarcely entered her narrative. New London's deep reliance on enslaved labor, on the slave-powered agriculture of the Caribbean, and even the city's connections to the trade in human beings in Africa did not have a place in the story she wanted to tell.

Perhaps it is safer to say that Caulkins did not see a way to integrate slave ownership—which she regarded as deeply wrong—with the history of townspeople and ancestors she genuinely admired and sought to venerate. Scholar David Blight has said that slavery is the piece of the American narrative that just doesn't "fit."

I found a truer picture of the role and ubiquity of New London's enslaved in the diary of Joshua Hempstead, which Hempstead maintained from 1711 until several weeks before his death in 1758. (Dudley Saltonstall, who was about to turn twenty, had returned from the third voyage in the logbooks the autumn that Hempstead died.) In that diary, the labor of slaves and a port immersed in slave-based agriculture in the West Indies breathe up from many pages. But in Joshua Hempstead's day and in Saltonstall's, slavery was, among New Londoners, not a subject for criticism, nor did it negatively influence a man's reputation.

In the New London both men inhabited, captive labor was part of the fabric of everyday life, perfectly legal, and extremely necessary. A city was being built, with its constellation of outlying farms and settlements, and there was more work to do than there were white hands to do it. There were houses, businesses, stone walls, and wharves to be built. Farms and shipyards and enterprises of every kind required hands to make them and tend them. The greatest need and the most pressing exigency of this new world was not human equality but labor.

A new world that was still an experiment when Joshua Hempstead's father was born in 1649 was on solid footing when Saltonstall boarded the *Africa* in 1757, and captive labor—those black human beings who appeared briefly or not at all in the histories being written—was the reason.

When Dudley was just a toddler, his family and that of Colonel Browne of Salem, Connecticut, whose large farm was worked by slaves, went with Joshua Hempstead out to a house party on nearby Fisher's Island, which was then leased to George Mumford. Mumford also owned captives on his island farm.

"The whole party crossed with Mr. Mumford in his sail-boat, and remained four days on the island, nobly entertained by the Mumford family," recounted Caulkins. There were entertainments and carriage drives and a great deer hunt, at which Dudley's father Gurdon brought down a doe, and George Mumford killed two bucks, "one of which was immediately dispatched by carriage to Mr. Wanton, of Newport, as a present from the party."

A prominent Rhode Island family, the Wantons were politicians and mariners with connections to slavery. In the last of the voyages in Dudley Saltonstall's logbooks, when he and his ship were captured by the French, Rhode Island commander Joseph Wanton, and his ship, the *Prince of Prussia*, were captured just before them. (Eventually, they all returned to New England together in Saltonstall's ship.)

For more than a century, New England's ruling-class families were deeply intertwined, and slavery was part of their everyday world. Few of them became active slave traders, but dependence on enslaved labor was a constant of their lives. Within a few years of the Mumfords' house party in 1739, the enslaved black man who would later create one of the most famous accounts of New England slavery began working on George Mumford's farm. He was not called Venture Smith then, but only Venture, the name given to him by Robertson Mumford aboard a Rhode Island slave ship leaving Africa and bound for the island of Barbados. When Venture and three other men ran away from George Mumford's Fisher's Island farm in 1754, Mumford offered twenty pounds for their return.

In her careful expression that "many families in town owned slaves, for domestic service, some but one; others two or three; very few more than four," Frances Caulkins was both admitting and denying. She was admitting that many local families owned slaves, but then she tried to minimize that presence: yes, they were here; yes, many owned them; but nobody owned too many. "Domestic service" does not suggest someone over whom the owner held—and could exercise—the power of life and death. It does not suggest, for instance, the kind of hard farm labor that Adam Jackson provided for thirty years to Joshua Hempstead and to other farmers on days when Hempstead loaned them his service. It does not suggest, as Hempstead noted in January of 1751, the situation of a small black girl named Zeno whose owners were questioned after she died of a beating.

Caulkins was presenting her own version of the classic "yes, but" argument that appears in many forms around American enslavement. Too good a historian not to admit that New London families owned slaves, she still sought to modify that captive presence and a system that, as an abolitionist, she knew to be so cruel that it had to be ended.

In the past ten years, I have often been reassured that slavery is an issue for the South to address, that the North wasn't really part of the story, and that the limited slavery that did exist in New England was too different to be regarded in the same light. But slavery is a landscape that you learn to see, and once you see it, it stays with you.

Slavery served white people in the North and the South, and the abolitionists of the North are not the other side—the equivalency—of what enslaved black men and women suffered in New England. When I looked for differences between Northern and Southern slavery, I found similarities. The killing uncertainties of life as a captive were linked to the state of bondage, not geography. White America has tried to disown the history and damage of slavery, but the harder we struggle, the more we are enmeshed.

Putting aside Frances Caulkins, I felt closer to her city's true story when I read issues of the eighteenth-century newspaper the *New-London Summary, or, The Weekly Advertiser*, with its cheerful and confident slogan,

"With The Freshest Advices Foreign and Domestick." The newspaper was founded in 1758, and reflects the era when Dudley Saltonstall was getting his sea legs.

A culture enmeshed in slavery emanates from the pages of the *Summary*. New London merchants sell molasses, spices, and "Muscovado" sugar, all products of the Caribbean where enslaved black people were worked, often to death, in an agricultural system understood even then to be a kind of hell.

The names of the local ships headed for and returning from the West Indies are listed in each week's edition. Slaves are for sale, and slaves run away. These slave sales, spices, ships, and sugars all appear as separate news items, and in separate parts of the newspaper, but they are part of a single, much larger narrative: the story of 12 million people bought and sold in the transatlantic slave trade.

This commerce was an integral part of the *triangle trade* involving Europe, the Americas, and Africa—a trade that actually had a few more corners than an actual triangle. Ships left Europe and North America carrying manufactured goods, which were then traded for slaves and raw materials in Africa. Slaves were carried to North America, the Caribbean, Suriname on the northern coast of South America, and Brazil, where they were traded for sugar, for sugar by-products such as molasses, and for spices. These products went back to the American colonies—where the molasses was distilled into huge quantities of rum—and to Europe. New England also shipped huge amounts of food and livestock directly to the Caribbean to sustain the plantation system where enslaved workers grew sugar for the Western Hemisphere. In a system that made a commodity of their human lives, black people were both the engine for growing the sugar and the object traded for it.

This circuit of trade made fortunes in Europe, in the Caribbean, and in America, where the labor of slaves helped transform a handful of colonies into a nation. Bernard Bailyn, a prominent scholar of New England's colonial history, has described slavery as "the key dynamic force" that propelled New England to early prosperity.

And by the early eighteenth century, the Connecticut port of New London had everything it needed to succeed in the triangle of trade, beginning with a population of seasoned mariners, skilled shipbuilders, and eager entrepreneurs. It also had one of the deepest natural harbors in the colony and a necklace of farming communities producing food, lumber, and premium livestock for export.

For a city as fully engaged in provisioning West Indies plantations as New London, Africa was the logical next step, and the pages of the *New-London Summary* provided testimony on that, too. "To be sold, A Negro Wench Just arrived from the Coast of Africa," read an advertisement in July 1761. (The *Summary* ceased publication in August 1763 but was revived later the same year under the name *New-London Gazette*, and continued to publish for a decade.)

As I began to learn of New London men and their voyages to Africa, the thriving Connecticut River port of Middletown—just a day's sail up the Connecticut River—emerged as part of the story because men from Middletown often sailed from New London. Though not a deep-water port like New London, Middletown was a city that also drew its lifeblood from trade, and was a vivid and bustling center of maritime commerce with wharfs, ropewalks, provisioners, and merchants all involved in the Caribbean trade.

I remembered those pages from the New London newspapers when I read, at the long research table in the Middlesex County Historical Society, the account books of Middletown merchants Samuel Willis and Samuel Starr. Willis, a sea captain who also managed a store, had business dealings throughout the Connecticut River Valley. He provisioned ships headed to the West Indies and Africa, and sold basic household goods such as tools, food, paint, and window glass, as well as imported goods such as ribbon, tea, coffee, and fine fabric. He also sold lots of rum to ships, to local residents, and even to himself.

In the book of Willis's figured-to-the-pence handwritten accounts covering 1765 to 1778, the comings and goings of a busy port are returned to life, and I read as Captain Easton, Captain Waterman,

Timothy Miller, Richard Alsop, and others provisioned their ships with kettles and rope, ship's bread and flour. A debt could be settled by "Continental mony," by a cask of "pimientos"—as allspice was then called—or by a gray horse. When Willis outfitted a "voyage to Carolina" in May of 1768, part of the bill was later settled "by ½ 5 Slaves cash 67.10," or a half interest in the value of five slaves, that half interest amounting to 67 pounds, 10 shillings.

Captain Timothy Miller was making his way up the Connecticut River with a cargo of enslaved people in the schooner *Speedwell* in 1763 when one of his crewmen grabbed an enslaved child and jumped overboard with her. "The vessel being under Sail they were both drowned," the *New-London Summary* reported on July 8, and the *Speedwell* continued on to Middletown. The seaman's body was recovered, but there was no mention of the little girl, who had, until then, survived so much.

From the upper windows of my little house just south of Middletown, I can see the river where she drowned.

Slaves directly from Africa were sold in both Middletown and New London. Two Middletown men traded in human beings so regularly that they are identified on an old map as slave dealers.

The histories of these cities contain much more than slavery, of course, but slavery is a part of both their stories. In both ports, the link between them and the coast of Africa is not a connection that *might* exist, but a relationship that we *know* existed because it is supported by documentation. This local history might be held in the shadows, rather like a silhouette of which we can see only the outline, but it is not shadowy. This is a history with names of men and ships, a history with details.

In a small Connecticut museum several years ago, I saw a map illustrating the triangle trade, showing solid lines connecting the port with islands in the British Caribbean where local ships had traded. Between the port and the west of Africa, there was only a dotted line, as if to suggest that a relationship *may* have existed.

The trade map in the museum represents a historical truth, a memory that cannot yet be taken into the port's local history, which is alive and cherished. The story of the logbooks and the men who were in the slave trade with Saltonstall, for instance, still has the power to wound. Looking for an old New London cemetery one day in late winter, I got lost and stopped in a job-training center to ask for directions. The job center is in an old red-brick public school, and I looked up to see the name Saltonstall carved in large letters over the main entrance. The first time I made a presentation on the logbooks in New London, the town historian approached me afterward and said, in a grieving way, "Are you sure?"

So much of New England's early history is so stirring and so guided by heroism and the common good, it is a consolation to think about it.

In 1961, Pulitzer Prize–winning novelist and poet Robert Penn Warren published a short and searching assessment of the Civil War and its legacy. On the subject of Northerners and their role in American slavery, he was scathing, and called the North's mistaken—and unshakable—notion of its own blamelessness "the Treasury of Virtue." "The Northerner feels redeemed, for he, being human, tends to rewrite history to suit his own deep needs; he may not, in fact, publish this history, but it lies open on a lectern in some arcane recess of his being, reading for his devotional perusal. . . . When one is happy in forgetfulness, facts get forgotten."

THE PAIN THAT SURVIVES

If we need to be convinced of how much memory
matters to us, we have only to ponder the fate
of someone deprived of its effective use.
EDWARD CASEY,
Remembering: A Phenomenological Study

My mother's forgetfulness made her miserable.

After her diagnosis of dementia, she seemed to want to stay at her home in West Hartford, where she had lived for forty years, and we arranged for a series of caregivers to live with her so that she would never be alone. Her favorite was a tall Jamaican woman named Retinella, Nella for short. Nella brought with her bags of spices and made wonderful meals. She had a beautiful way of saying my mother's name, *Dah*-ris, and they would take walks together in the neighborhood.

But Mama never understood who Nella was or why she was, as my mother said, "sleeping over." As Mama's deepening confusion began to outstrip even Nella's watchful and tender care, my brother and I started visiting assisted-living residences near our homes. We wanted to find someplace that would be cozy, a place where she would be surrounded by women her age and be safe, yet still have some privacy and have the chance to do things she enjoyed, like swimming and crafts.

I visited the Alzheimer's unit of an assisted-living facility that was nearby and had a few openings. Built on an old piece of farmland, the main building was big and elegantly decorated, the colors in the artificial flowers matching the color of the curtains. I took the tour and saw the private rooms and apartments for couples, and then I was taken into the dementia unit. It was like entering a warm, aggressively scented hive.

Elderly women were watching an old movie, or puttering in their rooms, or just walking up and down the long carpeted hallway. On the wall outside each resident's room was a box containing pictures from her life before old age and memory loss. In the photographs, young women with poufy, 1940s-style haircuts hugged soldier husbands and stood smiling in front of that small first house. There were daughters in braids, sons with butch-waxed crew cuts, and lots of Airedales and Scottie dogs.

The manager showing me around asked one of the residents if we could see her room, and she said, "Of course, I'm just tidying up!" For a moment, I had the sensation I was already in my mother's room, so recognizable were the woman's possessions: a crocheted afghan in harsh colors, the Martha Washington sewing cabinet, china figurines, and cheaply framed pictures of the grandkids.

The woman had a large dresser in her room, and on each drawer, she had pasted a large sticky note that read "Odds and Ends."

"Helps keep me organized," she said cheerfully.

As it happened, Mama did not move to the dementia wing for several years. Despite her diagnosis, because her manners and many of her life skills were intact, she was able to live in a wing with women who did not have dementia. She was cheerful, liked to help clear the table after meals, and most of the time seemed to think she was living in a very nice girls' school. She was part of a knitting group that made hats and mittens for indigent seamen—"Are you making this up?" my sister asked when I told her—and was regarded by the staff as a gentle influence on the other residents. The relatives of one resident were so moved by Mama's ability to manage their truculent matriarch that they included her in lobster feasts and outings for ice cream.

I stopped by one night after work, and as I walked into the main foyer, I heard Mama's laughter float down the main stairway that led to the floor where she lived. I went upstairs, and she was standing with a small group of women, all of them holding post-dinner cups of decaf. "Oh hello," my mother said, not able to summon my name. But another woman bailed her out and greeted me by name, so then she could. I had loved hearing her laugh.

But one day she put on a red straw hat and decided she would walk home to West Hartford. She stopped in a package store to ask for a map; luckily, a nurse's aide picking up a soda recognized her and suggested they walk back to the residence for Mama's purse, which she would need for her journey.

That was the end of her freedom.

Her new private room and bath were smaller, and though she did not object to the change, she seemed to lose ground. She kept taking down the paintings my brother had hung around her room. On her eightieth birthday, Mama wept and would not be consoled. She thought the "other girls" were being mean to her and begged me to stop by and visit her mother, who had died decades earlier. "You don't have to stay long, just say hello," she pleaded. I bought a notebook for her and wrote down names, dates, and facts that she could read for reassurance, forgetting, of course, that she could no longer read and why had a stranger given her this book?

I saw that I had not understood the true nature of her disease at all, and that forgetting her children's names or how to make a pumpkin pie were the very smallest and most benign parts of what was happening to her. Despite the warm cocoon we had arranged for her, Mama was going to suffer because she didn't know who *she* was. Losing her past made her disabled in the present and stole her future.

I had begun to read about the science of memory formation to better understand why America's long relationship with enslavement is so imperfectly understood, but Mama's once-beautiful face, now raddled by confusion and anxiety, was teaching me, too. She was losing her personal history, year by year, yet she remembered her childhood in upstate New York with piercing clarity, and badgered me to sign her up for summer camp.

I wondered why my country's historical memory seemed to work so differently from organic memory. Most commonly, dementia erases the most recent past, like whether you brushed your teeth or ate breakfast, and then moves inexorably through your bank of memories, removing husbands, children, learned skills, and basic realities along the way. My eighty-year-old mother didn't recognize me, but was looking forward to practicing archery and swimming to the float at Camp Friendly.

By contrast, New England's historical memory is more fragile and has more holes the farther back we go. We remember our shared history in a way that is not organic, and not in the way individual human beings remember and then forget. We say—and we believe—that we were great mariners, great farmers, and that we became rich by engaging in a global trade within a few decades of debarking in the early seventeenth century. That interpretation is accurate as far as it goes, but is so incomplete as to be untrue. When my mother thought we were fibbing as children, she would say, *Half the truth is a whole lie.*

Stolen labor helped to build New England; captive people in the Caribbean needed the food we grew and the livestock we raised. As shippers and trans-shippers in the vessels we built and navigated so well, we participated at every level of an enterprise that held the forced labor of black human beings at its heart. Their lives were the key to the strongbox. That's equally part of the story, and it is the part that makes our history whole, a history with integrity.

Why was New England's profound relationship with slavery, both in its numbers and commercial connections, so limited a part of the local narratives? Slavery's economic significance, its ubiquity and its cruelty, all thoroughly supported by documentation from the seventeenth, eighteenth, and nineteenth centuries, had been transformed in the history books into something so mild and gentle it barely needed to be mentioned, and often was not.

A disease had destroyed my mother's context for who she was, what she knew, and what she cared about. I wondered what had happened to my country, to have misplaced so much of its own early memory.

What my mother didn't know was hurting her. The idea that American enslavement was limited, not that bad, and that it *ended* with the Emancipation Proclamation of 1863, is as damaging to our nation as my mother's memory loss was to her. Her life after dementia was incomplete, as incomplete as the narratives of American history that are still written and still taught. I saw that the two stories—my mother's and my country's—could be examined and studied together, and that each would help me understand the other. In the wreckage of my mother's life and in the logbooks, I found clues to help me build a history that is not over, and that has depths still waiting to be explored.

There is a piece of advice that comes up often in families where there is dementia: "Join the journey." It means, don't try to reason with the dementia sufferer, because the sufferer cannot reason. Try instead to understand the feeling behind the person's actions, and then address that feeling. My mother's insistence on writing to her long-dead mother was a piece of very old and lifelong pain: that of trying to placate a bitter and unloving parent. Grandmother was dead, but the pain she had caused her daughter was still alive at Mama's eighty-year-old core.

Once I understood the pain inside my mother's many and varied anxieties—that she was unloved, had not been a good daughter, and would be destitute when her money was gone—I was able to be patient, and to help her deal with her suffering. Because she had no short-term memory and could not retain new information, her anxiety could never be mastered, but at least I had the tools to console her, even if she needed consoling several times a day.

Anthropologist Michael Jackson, who lived in Sierra Leone during the 1970s, wrote a memoir of his time there as a young ethnographer and of his return in 2002, after the country's long civil war. He writes, "Memories are like stories, constantly remade and refashioned, though we cling to the belief that they can be faithful to the events they recount. It is hard for us to admit the full extent to which our vision of the way things are is filtered, constructed, and distorted . . . And harder still, perhaps, to argue that what we finally come to see as 'reality' may still be illusory."

THE FRAGILE POWER

Except for those few individuals who are blessed—or cursed—with photographic memory, it is hard for us to be accurate when remembering events that happened a long time ago. Pioneering memory scientist Elizabeth Loftus found in her research that when we are presented with new information, we seek ways to connect it to what we already know, or to other information that seems to us likely or probable. Then we take these inferences, which we experience as facts, and connect them to other "facts," which may or may not be accurate. She has called this process of bridging gaps in our memory *refabrication,* noting that a fringe of untruth probably occurs in nearly all of our everyday reports of facts, not just reports of events that happened a long time ago. Stored as memories, these refabrications seem real to us, and we trust in their accuracy.

In his 2011 study of the lives of twenty people during World War I, historian Peter Englund writes that no one understands the whole story, and that the lack of hard information gets "padded out with guesses, suppositions, hopes, fears, idées fixes, conspiracy theories, dreams, nightmares and rumors."

We expect our memory to serve us in the way that our digital instruments do, and we have great confidence in the memories we build, but scientists say that what begins as memory and then becomes history is subject to so many internal and external pressures that those memories rarely survive whole. In the more than 150 years since William James began puzzling over how we remember, human memory has come to be understood as fraught, highly selective, and steered by individual interests and passions. Indeed—and this does not bode well for the objectivity of our recall—the most powerful governor of what we remember or forget is subjective interest, James calling this subjectivity "the very keel on which our mental ship is built."

Neurobiologist William Calvin says that we tend to see ourselves as the narrator of a life story, situated midway between past and future. "We can construct alternative explanations for how we got where we are, emphasizing one aspect or another as a path," he notes, adding that we do this as individuals and as a culture, too. From among the millions of memory bytes flooding our brains every day, we *choose*. The author of both scientific and laypeople's texts on the workings of primate and human brains, Calvin says, "A great deal of consciousness involves guessing well, as we try to make a coherent story of the fragments."

Memory research of the past fifty years has found that we tend to remember the gist of what we are told or shown, but not the details, and the details we miss can be striking. What we remember generally conforms to what we already know, or think we know, or what seems likely to be true. We see what we are expecting to see, or what we are asked to look for, and we are self-concerned interpreters of all incoming information, which tends to ensure that our memories will be faulty.

Psychologist and Nobel laureate Daniel Kahneman maintains that as human beings, we have an "exaggerated expectation" for the experiences of our lives to be consistent. "We are prone to think that the world is more regular and predictable than it really is, because our memory automatically and continuously maintains a story about what is going on, and because the rules of memory tend to make that story as coherent as possible and to suppress alternatives."

Shortly before beginning to write this book, I left a convenient, well-paying job with good benefits because I didn't think, at sixty, I would be able to learn a new set of skills. The job no longer required my traditional editing and writing skills, and was morphing into a position that demanded an interest in social media and a knowledge of the digital world I didn't have and didn't think I could build. I was afraid that if I stayed, I would be humiliated in my attempt to learn the new pieces of the job. I thought I would be bored, too, but I feared the potential for humiliation more. I told people that my job was eliminated—and that was true, but it wasn't the *truth* that I was also trying to protect myself and wanted very badly to leave. It was, however, a coherent version of what happened, and usually was accepted with a knowing nod. In 2011, lots of jobs were eliminated.

Kahneman, who won the Nobel Prize for economics in 2002, says that the confidence we feel in our stories comes from believing they are coherent, "and by the ease with which [they] come to mind, even if the evidence for [them] is sparse and unreliable."

We like to think of our memory as a kind of digital camera, able to show us a precise picture of what we saw, seconds later or whenever we choose to call up that information. But human memory is actually more like the snapshots we used to get back from the drugstore weeks after they were taken: a little out of focus, the frame containing more wallpaper than baby, and a feeling of vague disappointment, as in, *that wasn't what I saw.*

Darwin wouldn't have been surprised by those blurry 3"-by-5"s because, from an evolutionary point of view, it is not necessary for memory to be perfect. For us to be able to retrieve information with fidelity, there needs to be an adaptive advantage in remembering it, and for human beings, it seems possible that the adaptive advantage may be in maintaining the already coherent story and perhaps even in creating a story that is not wholly wrong but not truly faithful to the history that occurred. New England's history has been recontoured and made more pleasing to the senses—"We didn't have slaves here"—despite ample evidence that tells another story. (One of the audience questions I encountered often when making presentations on *Complicity* was, "What did the slaves *do*?" The national notion that black people were primarily agricultural workers hasn't made room for the reality that captive workers in the North did every kind of work—from baking to printing to sailmaking to shipbuilding to compounding medicines. They worked on farms, but they also worked as cooks, as cart drivers, as shopkeepers, and as dyers of cloth. They were not allowed to be judges or teachers or lawyers, but in New England, just about the *only* thing enslaved workers didn't do was grow cotton.)

Memory draws its truth from our feelings, and thus is linked to the deepest part of us. Harvard psychologist and researcher Daniel Schacter calls memory "the fragile power" because, despite its flawed formation, it has a profound influence on our thinking and actions. Memory is how we define ourselves as individuals and within our various cultures. Memory is powerful, and governs opportunity, social class, education, and values. The memory of who we are and where we come from shapes our lives.

It was considered a breakthrough when sociologists discovered that battered children often become violent parents, and that the children of alcoholics often marry alcoholics. The descendants of an enslaved and despised population are still despised—and disenfranchised—because that's the way memory *works*. It shapes and determines the present. Once we understand that, we can also understand why the lethal nature of American enslavement was not limited to the suffering and brutality it inflicted on generations of forcibly immigrated black people and their descendants, but also took the form of prejudice that went hand in hand with the institution itself. And it has lasted. Scholar Eric Williams, who examined the development of Caribbean slavery and its economic origins, emphasizes that the origin of black slavery "had not to do with the color of the laborer, but [with] the cheapness of the labor," and that cultural and physical differences of black people "made it easier to justify and rationalize" their enslavement. As slavery became more deeply entrenched in the United States, a labor system that had risen from capitalism and was seen by whites as necessary to their welfare became a system that was portrayed and viewed as beneficial and even necessary to the enslaved themselves, a profoundly damaging transformation.

For the majority of African Americans, their faces are evidence of something that happened. You cannot tell, by looking at my white face, whether my ancestors came over on the Mayflower nearly four centuries ago or on some stinking steamer during the nineteenth century. Actually, the latter is true, but my face doesn't say much about my background except that I'm probably of northern European ancestry. You cannot look at me and see that my ancestors were mostly poor people and that they struggled. On my father's side, I am separated from disabling poverty by only one generation, but you can't see that on my face.

A black face in the United States suggests that at some point in this person's family history, there was suffering, poverty, and discrimination. When colonial Americans created a slaveholding society in which the captive class was identifiable by color, they helped establish a national culture of race prejudice that has endured. The set of negative suppositions that white people attached to people of color—that, as a people, they were lazy, carnal, given to criminality, childlike, and incapable of caring for themselves—is alive today, still strong within modern culture.

Profound white prejudice about the personhood of black people, shaped by a misunderstood history, has created an America in which racial equality is still illusory. Black Americans are still poorer than whites, live shorter lives, have less access to good health care, are less likely to finish high school and go to college, and are less likely to own their own homes. They are less likely to have health insurance and more likely to be imprisoned. The median income of black families trails that of white families by thousands of dollars. That is the power of memory and the power of its loss.

In 2013, the United States celebrated the 150th anniversary of the Emancipation Proclamation. I attended speeches, dance programs, and readings, and came away feeling discouraged. I wondered why the white speakers were so quick to point to the more than a century and a half since emancipation, as if that made slavery, in some way, *over*. But in discussion groups led by African Americans, there was a note of despair, and a sense that racism may have become less overt, but it is alive and well.

Several years earlier, I had noticed that as frail as my mother's memory had become, she remembered the slights and hurts of eighty years before.

The descendants of Holocaust survivors often are deeply engaged by the effort to remember and record what their ancestors suffered, and the reality that they are descended from people intended for complete annihilation matters to them. It is part of who they are as human beings. Would it not also be legitimate for black Americans today to internalize and remember the centuries of what their ancestors suffered, and the decades of racism that have followed? Wouldn't that still be part of who they were and are? Suffering beyond quantification or measure has a particular kind of legacy, one that does not recognize boundaries as fragile as time and place. For white Americans, too, there is a story waiting to be heard.

In twenty years of reporting on postwar Germany for the *New Yorker*, Jane Kramer discovered a shift in the thinking of modern Germans, and "a kind of ultimate revisionism . . . an end-of-the-past project that was turning the twelve dark years of Hitler into twelve years of resistance *to* Hitler and occupation *by* Hitler; an abandonment, for the sake of settling the past into 'history,' of the very plain historical truth that Germany had *chosen* Hitler."

In a haunting book about how ordinary Germans willingly partic-

As he helped to clear jungle growth from the ruins on Bence Island, a man from neighboring Tasso Island was profiled in an upper window. This slave-trading fortress was the last of as many as six slave trading castles built on the island over the course of more than a century. Courtesy of Tom Brown/*Hartford Courant*

Danish slave ship captains traded at Bence Island, and this Danish-made cannon, believed to date from about 1780, lies tangled in the roots of the jetty where Europeans and colonials arrived for trade and Africans departed from their homeland. Courtesy of Tom Brown/*Hartford Courant*

When the island's ruins were, essentially, rediscovered in 1947 by Sierra Leonean physician M. C. F. Easmon, the ruins were engulfed by vegetation, and even today the jungle moves quickly to reclaim them. Courtesy of Tom Brown/*Hartford Courant*

It is impossible to see the ruins of the slaving fortress and not imagine what captive people would have felt when they first saw it. This structure was designed to suggest prosperity to the larger world, and fear to the Africans. Courtesy of Tom Brown/*Hartford Courant*

During the era when Connecticut men visited Bence Island for trade, the work of guarding and feeding the people being held for trade was done by black workers called *grommetos*. Through these two doorways, grommetos would have carried in food for the captives and carried out their waste. The women and children were held in rooms that once stood at the upper left of the enclosure. Men were held, chained and naked, in the larger open space. Courtesy of Tom Brown/*Hartford Courant*

A guarded gatehouse once surmounted this main doorway to the fortress. The fortress itself was a center for a trade, a place where to-be-sold human beings were warehoused, and a prison for them as they waited to be sold. Courtesy of Tom Brown/*Hartford Courant*

Bence Island is the smallest in an archipelago of islands that were involved in the slave trade, and where men from Europe and the American colonies traded for captured people who were then sold as laborers in the New World. Courtesy of Tom Brown/*Hartford Courant*

Today, the Bence Island of the logbooks is called Bunce Island, and the island has been abandoned for nearly two centuries. Many of the people who live on the neighboring islands are fishermen. Courtesy of Tom Brown/*Hartford Courant*

Braima Bangura is the caretaker of Bunce Island, and lives on a nearby island called Pepel. Mr. Bangura accompanies visitors to the island, and maintains a large scrapbook of their names. Courtesy of Tom Brown/*Hartford Courant*

In Sierra Leone's national museum in the capital of Freetown, a small handmade model evokes the struggle of the Sierra Leonean captives aboard a Spanish-built slave ship called *La Amistad*. Later to become a powerful symbol in the antislavery movement, the Mende people revolted and took over the ship. Courtesy of Tom Brown/*Hartford Courant*

When Joseph Opala visited Bunce Island in 2004, he found this piece of jaw-bone emerging from earth near the island's shoreline. With the permission of the government of Sierra Leone, Joe brought the piece of bone to the United States, where it was identified as between 200 and 300 years old, and as the jawbone of a child. Courtesy of Tom Brown/*Hartford Courant*

ipated in the attempt to annihilate Jewish people, Daniel Jonah Goldhagen writes that the Holocaust defies explanation using the ordinary
tools that human beings have to "explain" history, and that to understand an event without parallel in modern history, one must recon-
ceive the Germany of the day, anti-Semitism as it then existed, and
the Germans themselves. Otherwise, this impossible event cannot be
understood, and we will forever be mired in a "general lack of knowledge and all kinds of misunderstandings and myths."

We like to believe that history is an independent body of facts that
we neither shape nor influence, as if it were not a record that we ourselves create. History is a human product, less a record of what happened than many versions of what happened, brought together and
given the label "history." But the human perceptions that created that
history function in the service of self-interest, and the primary purpose
of memory, scientists say, is not accurate recall but self-protection. If
you study the mechanics of memory, it seems that forgetting is what
we do best. When we bury or set aside ideas that are frightening or
shaming, or that make us uncomfortable, we're doing what comes nat-
urally, and research of the past sixty years has demonstrated just how
flawed memory is.

In *Hitler's Willing Executioners: Ordinary Germans and the Holocaust*,
Goldhagen argues that if we think of the Germans of that era as following a basic template for human behavior and as basically "rational,
sober children of the Enlightenment," we will never understand why
relatively modern, twentieth-century Germans participated so fully in
a genocide against, among others, fellow Germans who happened also
to be Jewish. We need to understand the nature of their anti-Semitism
to begin to grasp what followed.

American colonists also were a post-Enlightenment society. To
understand how a modern democracy founded on the ideals of personal liberty became the world's largest slave society requires a similar "going back" so that we can look at the thinking of the time. Even
as it expanded and became more essential to the national economy,

American enslavement was surrounded by the "lack of knowledge" and "myths" cited by historian Goldhagen.

Even during the two centuries when it was being lived, slavery wasn't seen for the instrument that it was. Slaves appear in the New England records as "servants," and were widely believed to be an inferior kind of people. "Pretends to be free" was an expression that appeared often in the advertisements for runaway slaves, as if freedom for a black man or woman could exist only as a pretense, as if they were designed to be enslaved. Colonials understood that a black skin signaled enslavement and an inherent inferiority, though enslaved black workers were valuable, skilled, necessary, and sexually desirable.

Few helpers appear more often than Joshua Hempstead's slave Adam Jackson, who is a frequent presence in his diary of eighteenth-century New London, and who worked side by side with Hempstead for thirty years. They took care of each other—Joshua when he was sick with the flux and Adam when he was drunk—but Joshua Hempstead was a propertied white man, and Adam Jackson was his slave. Though he is not listed in Hempstead's will, his name appears at the end of an inventory that was added: "An old negro man named Adam, value [two pounds]." Scholar Allegra di Bonaventura found that Adam Jackson did become a free man, though he stayed poor and did not live to become old.

Jackson, whose ancestors had been in colonial Connecticut for almost as long as Hempstead's, was a black man living during the first half of the eighteenth century, and no social scale of that era would have made him the human equivalent of his white owner.

I thought of the experiences of African-born Venture Smith, who survived years of New England enslavement to become a free man and prosperous. He owned land on the Connecticut River, houses, and boats, and his son Cuff fought on the side of the colonists during the American Revolution, but he knew that justice was ephemeral for black people. Prosecuted for a barrel of molasses that another man had lost from a boat Smith owned, Smith said that such an action "would in my native country have been branded as a crime equal to highway robbery. But Captain Hart was a *white gentleman,* and I a *poor African,* therefore it was *all right, and good enough for the black dog."* The italics are Venture's, and you can hear his rage. Though he is often presented as a success story because of his later prosperity, his bitterness asks to be heard.

Neuroscientist Eric Kandel, whose family fled the Nazis when he was eight-and-a-half and who won the Nobel Prize for his work on the biology of memory, believes that even in a culture with high-quality ideas and ideals—such as the Vienna of his childhood—respect for human life cannot be assumed. "Culture is simply incapable of enlightening people's biases and modifying their thinking," he writes, adding that "the desire to destroy people outside the group to which one belongs may be an innate response."

le Imploy'd abo rigging Carp.r & Joiner making awning
er Making a Pump Can No Trade at all ___

rday July 15.th 1758 this 24 hours Light Winds & pleas.t Wea.r
e Imploy'd over hawling Blocks Carp.r & Joiner Making
ng ___ No Trade only Bought Some Corn & plantins

ay July 16.th this 24 hours Light Winds & pleas.t Wea.r People
y'd abo.t Jobs Carp.r & Joiner abo.t the awning the Cap.t or
Wanton No Trade Purchased one boy Slave of Quaquom

day July 17. this 24 hours Light Winds & pleas.t Wea.r Peo,
loy'd over hawling tobacco Carp.r & Joiner abo.t the awning
ade at all ___ Sail'd for Sirrenam the Large Dutch S
500 & od Slaves onboard ___

ay July 18. this 24 hours Light Winds & pleas.t Wea.r People
y in y.e Hold & fetching Brazeal Tobacco from a Dute
Cap.t Buley ___ Purchased one man Slave ___

esday July 19. this 24 hours Light Winds but a Large s
le Imploy'd picking Tobacco No Trade at all ___

day July 20. this 24 hours Calm & little Wind People Implo
Hold Cooper a Cutting Rum H.d Purchased one Two Slave
selsely in y.e Rhode except three Poor Rum Men ___
d the yaul up to Clean ___ broacht a bt Bee

y July 20 this 24 hours Calm Weather People Imploy'd ove
old & found a Hogs.d N.o 86 Leaked all out N.o 85 only 54 Gal.s in
gin to y.e Cap.t ___ Leakage ocationed by all y.e Head Hoops fly
rade this 24 hours ___ the Cap.t agri'd with my Lord to Send a man
to accraw after y.e Longboat for 4 Gal.s Trade Rum ___

rday July 21.st this 24 hours Calm Wea.r People Imploy'd f
heads with Water & with Rum Cooper a Cutting Hogs
d from y.e Longboat by a Letter from Understood u
g at Mumford with 3 Slaves on board ___

nday July 23.d this 24 hours Calm & hazey Weather at 10
be Ship to W.d Ward which we Suppos'd to be the English Man of

FOUR

A History That Doesn't "Fit"

BACK TO AFRICA

Each life, put out, lies down within us.
GALWAY KINNELL

Fifteen months after that first voyage aboard the *Africa* in January 1757, Dudley Saltonstall sailed out of New London harbor into an afternoon of rain and gale winds aboard a ship called the *Fox*. He was nineteen, and about to begin his chronicle of the third voyage in the logbooks, having already served as the chief mate on two slaving voyages, and having experienced, at close hand, the Guinea trade. He had become a rum man, as he himself referred to Africa traders, and was again on his way to buy slaves in West Africa, sailing on a ship that his father Gurdon owned and representing his father's interests on board.

For this voyage aboard the *Fox* in March 1758, William Taylor, a veteran slave ship captain based in Newport, Rhode Island, was in command. Taylor seems to have had a more cautious nature than bold Captain Easton, but he was successful enough to command vessels for Samuel and William Vernon, well-known Newport merchants, and he sailed at least twice on New London ships owned by Gurdon.

And in the oddly miraculous way that a single document about a long-ago voyage has settled in one place, an old newspaper account in another, and a log of the voyage itself in a third, Gurdon's sailing instructions for Taylor's voyage aboard the *Fox* have survived in an archive in Pawtucket, Rhode Island.

The sailing orders are dated March 24, 1758, and direct Taylor "to embrace the first fair Wind & proceed for the Coast of Africa, & endeavor to fall upon the Coast about Five Leagues to the Northward of Cape Mount." In a flowing and legible hand that strongly resembles Dudley's, Gurdon encouraged Taylor to sell his cargo "& invest the Nett Proceeds in good Slaves or Gold Dust or what you may Judge will best serve my interest." From the African coast, Taylor was to sail to the island of St. Christopher's, where Gurdon would leave further instructions for him with a merchant named John Wettet. If that plan were to fail, Taylor "must dispose of his Slaves for good Sterling Bills of Exchange & endeavor to get a Load of Molasses."

And if "by the Providence of God, you are renderd incapable to do the Business of this Voyage, then your Mate Mr. Dudley Saltonstall is hereby authoris'd & orderd to do the Same in manner & form as you are herein directed."

Four days later, with a crew of eleven men and one boy, five swivel guns, seven muskets, and two cutlasses for protection, the *Fox* sailed out of New London harbor.

After a fifty-one-day crossing filled with Saltonstall's notations of gales, fresh "breises," the men at their tasks, sightings of birds, casks of mackerel and beef being opened, and the occasional officers' meal of roasted fowl, the *Fox* reached Cape Mount, a beautiful high promontory on the very northern tip in what today is Liberia, and an established center for trade. Saltonstall mentioned that three canoes came off the shore for trade, but because a trader named Peter James had apparently bought a black trader's slaves and then snatched the trader, too, in the violation of trading practice called a panyar, "Capt. Taylor thought it not safe to trade."

For the next week, the *Fox* sailed a stretch of the Liberian coast that was punctuated with trading centers and the operations of freelance traders. Two English traders and a Frenchman were recommended to

Captain Taylor as very honest men, although within the week Salton-stall described the three as "Very Great Villians," for they made "no returns" on the rum and tobacco consigned to them for sale.

Cape Montserado, or Mesurado as it was also spelled, was a vital trading center at the mouth of St. Paul's River and today is the site of Monrovia, the capital of Liberia. Liberia was established by the American Colonization Society in an attempt to send free black Americans to Africa, and its capital was named for James Monroe, the fifth president of the United States, a slaveholder, and an ardent supporter of the largely unsuccessful Colonization Movement. (Few political moments speak more powerfully to the nation's insoluble division over slavery than the colonization program. It targeted for removal from American society not the enslaved millions, but free black citizens who, despite the extraordinary difficulties they faced in antebellum America, were ably refuting racist doctrine about black inferiority.)

Saltonstall's logbooks contain brief descriptions of the beautiful coastline, its clear hills and mountains gently sloping down to rivers and the sea. This was the Grain Coast to which his father Gurdon had directed them in his sailing instructions of two months earlier. A valuable pepper plant was grown here called *malaguetta*, or "grains of paradise." Rice was for sale at either ten hands of tobacco plus one basket, or one gallon of rum. Fresh water was plentiful on shore, and the wind was soft and fresh. The *Fox* sailed southward in company with a ship from Liverpool, then the center of England's slaving trade, toward the River Cestos, which the log keeper refers to as the River Sistors. They sailed all the way past modern-day Liberia and the Ivory Coast before sailing northeast at Cape Three Points, toward land and what today is Ghana.

Before parting company with the *Fox*, the commander of the Liverpool ship pointed them in the direction of Elmina Castle, a fifteenth-century trading fortress built by the Portuguese but under Dutch rule since the 1640s. Saltonstall described passing the "Mine Castles"—they are "abot a gunshot" apart—and then their ship, seventy-seven days from New London, was in the Anomabu Rhode and facing Cape Coast Castle.

The "rhode" or "road," as it was called, was the stretch of water where ships could safely anchor, out of reach of the dangerous rocks and rolling surf, and send their longboats ashore for water, provisions, and trade. Every trading center had a rhode, and it was also a place where ships' officers would socialize with each other and share information about trade, dangerous areas, tribal conflicts, and sightings of friends' vessels. During their next ten days at anchor in the Anomabu Rhode, Taylor and Saltonstall visited and dined with several other officers from New England, one of whom was headed for Jamaica and then home, and agreed to take a letter home to Dudley's father.

Situated on the center of the coast of modern Ghana—and so close to Elmina Castle that the onshore drive today takes only minutes— Cape Coast Castle was the center of British slave trade operations in West Africa. On old maps, this region is sometimes labeled the Gold Coast, because Europeans had mined gold since the late fifteenth century, and gold dust was a frequent article of trade. On June 17, the day after Saltonstall had paid the port customs fee and traded several gallons of rum for "one Boy Slave," he made a trade for "Some Gold."

In the next three days, Saltonstall purchased four more slaves, one of them a woman from "C.C.C."—his shorthand for Cape Coast Castle. Two Rhode Island ships stocked with captives headed for the plantations on Jamaica and in South Carolina, and a Dutch ship with 500 slaves on board headed for Suriname, where enslaved people grew cotton, cocoa, coffee, and sugar for the European market on an estimated 200 plantations.

Without self-consciousness, the logbooks render a detailed and perfect portrait of something that no longer exists. At once telegraphic and evocative, the logbooks sweep their light across the long ago. Dudley Saltonstall was not writing to document the colonial era slave trade of the mid-eighteenth century. He was keeping track of things for his father, as on July 20, 1758, when he noted, "No trade this 24 hours & the Capt. agreed with my Lord to send a man to Accraw [the port of Accra] after ye Longboat for 4 Gal. Trade Rum."

By July of 1758 when the *Fox* was anchored in the Anomabu Rhode, England and France had been at war for two years and two months as part of a larger, international conflict that is now called the Seven Years' War. Today considered an early world war because of the number of nations involved, the Seven Years' War consisted of one group of European allies against another; and on North American colonial soil, where it took shape as the French and Indian War, the English and the French fought over land. In international waters, French and British ships harassed each other, stealing cargo and capturing ships and crewmen.

Captain Taylor and Dudley Saltonstall were coping with the slow pace of trade and the discovery that hogshead number 86, a barrel containing about sixty-five gallons of rum, had leaked its entire contents when, on July 23, they spotted a ship to windward. In the heat and the haze, they guessed that it was an English man-of-war, but it proved instead to be a French man-of-war called the *Count Saint Florentine.* Armed with sixty guns on carriages, the ship, which had been outfitted by a group of merchants in Bordeaux, was functioning as a privateer and captured the much smaller *Fox.* Privateers were privately owned and outfitted vessels authorized by their government to attack and take enemy ships; later in his career, Dudley Saltonstall became a successful privateering captain.

Saltonstall's logbook did not resume for two weeks, but what happened next became the subject of New England newspaper stories and a lawsuit.

The *Count Saint Florentine*, with a crew of 550 men, had already captured two other ships and crews, including the sloop *King of Prussia,* under the command of Joseph Wanton of Rhode Island, and a snow called *Anamaboa*, with a Newport commander named Walter Buffam at the helm. A dramatic news account datelined Newport and published in the *Pennsylvania Journal* on October 26, 1758, recounted that after

Friday July 14th 1758 — this 24 hours Light Winds & pleas.t Wea.r
People Imployd abo.t rigging Carp.r & Joiner making awning 78
Cooper Making a Pump Can — No Trade at all

Saturday July 15th 1758 this 24 hours Light Winds & pleas.t Wea.r
People Imployd over hawling Blocks Carp.r & Joiner making
awning — No Trade only Bought Some Corn & plantins —

Sunday July 16th this 24 hours Light Winds & pleas.t Wea.r — People
Imployd abo.t Jobs Carp.r & Joiner abo.t the awning the Cap.t on
board Wanton Norton Purchased one boy Slave of Quaquominyus

Monday July 17. this 24 hours Light Winds & pleas.t Wea.r People
Imployd over hawling tobacco Carp.r & Joiner abo.t the awning —
No trade at all — Sailed for Surrenam the Large Dutch Ship
with 500 Odd Slaves on board —

Tuesday July 18. this 24 hours Light Winds & pleas.t Wea.r People
Imploy in y.e Hold & fetching Brazical Tobacco from a Dutch
now Cap.t Bailey — Purchased one man Slave —

Wednesday July 19. this 24 hours Light Winds but a Large Sea
People Imployd picking Tobacco No Trade at all —

Thursday July 20. this 24 hours Calm & little Wind People Imployd
y.e Hold Cooper a Cutting Rum it hd Purchased Two Slaves —
the Vessely in y.e Rhode except three Poor Rum Men
hoised the yaul up to Clean — braught a bt Beef

Friday July 20 this 24 hours Calm Weather People Imployd over hauls
Cooper y.e Hold & found a Hogs. N.o 86 Leaked all out N.o 85 only 54 Gal.n in both
belong in to y.e Cap.t — Leakage ocationed by all y.e Head Hoops flying
No trade this 24 hours — the agre'd with my Lord to Send a man by
Land to accraw after y.e Longboat for 4 Gal.r Trade Rum

Saturday July 22.d this 24 hours Calm Wea.r People Imployd fitting
Hogsheads with Water & with Rum Cooper a Cutting Hogs
heard from y.e Longboat by a Letter from Underwood who is
lying at Mumford with 3 Slaves on board —

Sunday July 23.d this 24 hours Calm & hazey Weather at 10th
Large Ship to W. Ward which we Supposd to be the English Man of War
from Goerea but provd to be a french Ship of War Cauld the
the Saint florintine of 60 Carriage Guns belonging to Bourdox
who made Prisoners of us —

the *Florentine* had snared the three New England ships, it was, in turn, attacked by two English ships, the *Harwich* with fifty guns and the *Rye* with twenty. The Englishmen cut the privateer's anchor cables, and when the French ship "endeavored to make her Escape," a firefight ensued that lasted for three hours.

On August 1, pieces of the French ship, including gun carriages, doors, and cannon tools bearing fleur-de-lis, began to wash ashore, "which made it conjectured the Privateer was either taken or sunk."

Gurdon Saltonstall brought suit against William Taylor in 1758, possibly because he had insurance on the vessel or the valuable trade goods on board the *Fox* when she was captured. In a Newport courtroom before a notary in October of that year, Taylor testified that when his ship was captured, he had on board five ounces of gold dust, thirteen slaves, seventeen rolls of tobacco, and between seventy and eighty hogsheads of rum. His ship and cargo were sold by the French commander to the governor of Coromantine Castle, a Dutch-owned fort a few miles from Cape Coast Castle. It is not clear what happened to the gold, rum, tobacco, and slaves, but Taylor testified that the governor of the Dutch castle sold the *Fox* to the governor of the fort at Anomabu, also nearby. Joseph Wanton and Walter Buffam, the two other Rhode Island captains who lost their ships and cargoes in the same incident as William Taylor, made sworn statements before the same notary on the same day. The making of these statements was the standard procedure when a captain suffered damage to his vessel, lost cargo to a storm or misadventure, or lost the vessel entirely, and provided the starting point for claims against the insurers of the cargo or

opposite:

On July 23, 1758, William Taylor and Dudley Saltonstall's ship, a snow called the *Fox*, was captured by a French privateering vessel called the *Count Saint Florentine*. Although the ship was returned to them later that summer, the tobacco, barrels of rum, gold dust, and thirteen slaves were confiscated. Logbooks, Courtesy of the Connecticut State Library the vessel. After its safe return from Africa, the *Fox* was sold in New-port to settle expenses the unfortunate voyage had incurred, so Gur-don Saltonstall must have reckoned this one on the loss side of the ledger.

The slaving castles, as scholar William St. Clair has pointed out, were not really castles, but heavily armed and defended warehouses that stored trade goods, including human beings, for sale. The gov-ernor was the man at the top, dictating terms, entertaining traders, and managing the infrastructure of a place that was a trading center, national outpost, barracks, and prison. The governor of Anomabu at that moment was Richard Brew, a bluntly spoken Irishman who had emigrated from Europe in the early 1750s. He made a career working for the British and later as an independent trader in a castle he built and named for himself. Brew returned the *Fox* to Taylor's command, so that "[I] might be enabled to return home and bring with [me] a Number of other British subjects who likewise had the Misfortune to be taken by the French Privateer," as Taylor later testified.

On board the *Fox* for the return trip to New England was Joseph Wanton, a familiar player in the slave trade and related to Saltonstall by marriage. Believed to have been the model for the portly drunk in John Greenwood's famous eighteenth-century painting of slave ship captains carousing in Suriname, Wanton was elected governor of Rhode Island in 1769.

After learning that Richard Brew had returned the *Fox* to Taylor and Saltonstall, allowing them to sail home with, at least, their ship intact, I read about Brew and his career. He was a man who lived in the slave trade up to his neck, and he was impatient with the niceties traders tried to impose on a brutal business that he knew to be brutal.

Married to the daughter of a local African leader who had prom-ised to support English trade interests and then made overtures to the French, Brew wrote, "And how could it be otherwise? The nature of the trade excludes what we call affection. The negroes know we would buy every one of them if we could sell them again."

Taylor lost his cargo in Africa, and Wanton lost his ship, as well as 124 hogsheads of rum and 54 slaves. But they were "treated with great Hospitality by the Gentlemen on the Coast," according to one account, and sailed for home on August 7.

After only four additional days of notations, Saltonstall's logbook for the *Fox* ends abruptly on August 10. The last page is ruled off, as if he meant to write more, and bears the heading "Africa towards New England." Perhaps, with this voyage, there was nothing more to say.

The men who helped to underwrite and hoped to profit from the slaving voyages in the logbooks—men like Dudley Saltonstall's father Gurdon, and Nathaniel Shaw of New London, whose stone house is now home to the city's historical society—knew that the dangers of the trade were many, and that even the ordinary perils of slaving were not ordinary. In 1755, slave merchant Henry Laurens wrote to the company owners of a slave ship called the *Gambia*, "Incidents are very common in the Africa business, against which everyone that enters upon it should fortify themselves." On his first three voyages, Dudley Saltonstall, not yet twenty, had survived violent storms in the Atlantic, a hard-driving captain, an outbreak of the bloody flux, and capture by the French.

Records of the mid-eighteenth century show Connecticut slave ship officers dying of fevers, or being murdered by African traders or by their own crew. Other lethal possibilities included drowning in storms and being mauled by wild animals while ashore. At a trading post in Cape Three Points in 1721, an African king directed English Navy surgeon John Atkins's attention to the lower jawbones of several Dutch traders, hanging from a tree limb, as if to illuminate what could happen in an unsuccessful trade relation.

In August 1764, the *New-London Gazette* reported that Captain Timothy Miller, a Middletown man whose name is embroidered throughout the records of the period, "bro't advice of the Death of Captain Joseph Miller, late Master of a small Sloop from this Port, and all his Hands except two, and that the Negroes, soon after, availing themselves of that Opportunity, came off from the Shore and killed the Two surviving Men, took Possession of and pillaged the Vessel." This occurred in Sierra Leone near Bence Island.

That same year, Commander Thomas Goold of the *Hope*, a ship owned by the Forseys of New London, died on the African coast when his chief mate and an accomplice crushed his head with musket blows and threw his body overboard. Chief Mate William Preest insisted that the captives on board had committed the murder, but then the slaves *did* rise against the small crew, and by the time Preest died in a Boston jail, he had confessed all.

Saltonstall was off on a voyage of his own in 1768 when his cousin Nathaniel, also a sea commander, was returning from Jamaica in company with a Newport ship owned by the Wanton family. The two ships were off the coast of Delaware in a thunderstorm when a bolt of lightning hit the Newport ship and "set Fire to a Quantity of Rum and Spirits between Decks," the *Providence Gazette* reported. The fire quickly spread, engulfing the vessel, and because the two ships were in "a heavy sea running," Saltonstall could not help the blazing ship and its passengers, all of whom perished.

Late that same year, the *New-London Gazette* published an account of Captain Turrel's report that the trade on the coast of Gambia "is greatly embarrassed and interrupted by the behavior of the natives, who make every attempt in their power to destroy the English." This interruption in trade had been occasioned by a disagreement between the governor of an English slaving fort and the local African king, and forced the colonists to arm themselves to the teeth.

Dudley Saltonstall lived in New London for most of his life, and he would have known the Millers, and also Thomas Goold. He would have known William Wignall, a New London captain who was killed when the captives on board his ship revolted on the coast of Africa in 1791.

The logbooks that Saltonstall kept, and which illuminate part of Connecticut's role in the slaving trade, conclude in August 1758, the year he turned twenty. He spent the next thirty-five years at sea in the West Indies trade, and for a few years was an officer in the Continental Navy. During the war, he had risen to commodore before the Battle of Penobscot Bay in Maine, a disastrous 1779 engagement in which Saltonstall, who was outgunned and outmanned by the experienced

British fleet, hesitated to engage with the enemy until it was too late. In the rout he lost all of his ships, and was later court-martialed aboard the *Deane*, a ship named for his brother-in-law, the influential Connecticut merchant, lawyer, and diplomat Silas Deane. (Deane was married to Saltonstall's sister Elizabeth.)

A moving letter by a man under Saltonstall's command, Captain Jonathan Parsons of Massachusetts, defends his commander's actions, and at least one modern scholar maintains that Saltonstall was made a scapegoat by Congress for the catastrophic loss, which the Massachusetts Board of War then estimated at more than 1 million pounds.

The few surviving descriptions of Dudley Saltonstall's nature come from men who served with him during the Revolutionary War, and they are not flattering. John Paul Jones, who would become much more famous than his commander, served as Saltonstall's lieutenant aboard the warship *Alfred*, and complained of his "Rude Unhappy Temper." As a New England aristocrat, Saltonstall probably had little in common with the majority of the 220 seamen aboard the *Alfred*, but Jones complained that he treated even his officers "as tho they were of a lower Species."

Saltonstall enjoyed the kinds of preferment and opportunities that often come to the children of high-born families, so when he lost his command, another opportunity presented itself in the form of a privateer outfitted for him by the brother of his wife Frances. Adam Babcock equipped the *Minerva* for Saltonstall, "That you might regain the character with the world in which you have been most cruelly and unjustly robbed of," according to a history written of the Saltonstall family. Late in the American Revolution, and after his court-martial from the Continental Navy, Saltonstall captured two English ships in 1781, one of them carrying a cargo valued at 80,000 pounds and one of the greatest prize ships of the war.

The prize ship, the HMS *Hannah*, was still anchored in New London in September of that year when American-born Benedict Arnold, at the head of a British regiment, set a fire that destroyed much of New

London's waterfront and many of its early houses, including the house where Dudley had grown up and that of his grandfather, early colonial minister and governor Gurdon Saltonstall.

In the space of those few hours on September 6, 1781, Arnold's fires destroyed dozens of businesses and homes, and more than a century of customs records as well as the early papers of the Saltonstalls, who had been in New London for nearly 100 years. On a day when New London's gutters were said to have run with rum and melted Irish butter, Arnold, whose name in this country has become a synonym for traitor, also unmoored the *Hannah* and made her a fire ship that drifted into other ships and burned them, too.

Published sources say that Saltonstall later "dabbled" in the slave trade, but a collection of business records and letters auctioned in Portsmouth, New Hampshire, in August 2013 show an involvement in the trade that was deeper than that.

Dudley Saltonstall, who was a ship's captain by 1762, the year he turned twenty-four, was a West Indies trader and involved in the trade with Africa until nearly the end of his life. In April 1784, he wrote to his wife Frances that he was at Anomabu on the coast of what today is Ghana and had acquired thirty slaves. He hoped to purchase another 300 captives, he wrote, and then planned to sail to South Carolina in July or August. He wrote to Frances again the following February from Charleston, where he had sold about half of his human cargo, and said the trade was so slow that he didn't know when he would be home.

The auctioned documents cover the years from 1762 to 1793, three years before Saltonstall's death, and show a busy and experienced mariner shipping wine, molasses, spermaceti candles, and captives around the Atlantic world. He appears to have flourished.

And what seems most interesting about Dudley Salstonall is neither his marriage to the daughter of a prominent Rhode Island physician and politician and the family they created, nor his disgrace in the Continental Navy and later redemption as a successful privateer and trader. The piece of his story that now seems most critical is the one that did not make it into the history books: the story of a young man aboard ships that sailed into the slave trade's vanished past. Saltonstall's logbooks are a chance to see him at the beginning, before he was disgraced or successful, or anything but the stripling son of a famous family, and to see, day by day, the terrible trade in which he helped to change a hemisphere.

NOT A WORD BUT A WORLD

Exploring enslavement in New England began as an assignment, one of the many I had during my newspaper life. And in real terms, it has become my last assignment, the one I can never finish or be parted from. Because my parents were idealists, and my siblings and I were encouraged to show good character in our actions, I grew up believing that my life should be *for* something. I thought I would find that something as a young woman, not at fifty-one, but the raw material of New England slaveholding was so gripping that I couldn't get past it, and it made my earlier work on gracious living and beautiful gardens seem insubstantial. The stories of the captives pulled me forward and then broke open my heart, and they were everywhere—in newspapers, court records, diaries, and census lists. An advertisement for a runaway black man who fled with a coarse brown coat and his violin. A man who said his twenty-five-year-old slave Pegg had fits and was so useless he would swap her "for a dead Negro." A teenager named Phillis who was sold in Middletown with a cow.

I wanted to protect them, and could do nothing for them except write, but their lives led me to the logbooks.

Names and places that had once been totally unfamiliar became part of a world that I could imagine because Saltonstall's logbooks and the eighteenth-century records that support them have a cinematic quality. I learned that the officers drank a potent punch made from brandy, rum, water, and sugar, and even the everyday records contain evocative descriptions of this drink, which was imbibed at every opportunity. In his 1744 account, cartographer William Smith described being welcomed to Sierra Leone by an Englishman named Captain Crocker. Smith's ship, having run out of limes, could offer the captain only Madeira wine in welcome, so Crocker sent to his vessel for "a handkerchief of limes and, whilst we drank Punch together, he gave us a short Account of the State of the Company's affairs at Bence Island."

Colonial traders were in a world so different from their own, they could not help remarking on its vivid and foreign nature. By the time I read that Saltonstall and a few seamen hauled aboard a sea turtle on March 15, 1757, only to discover that it was dead and "stunke bitterly," I had learned that turtle soup was a delicacy of the West Indies trade, and had seen recipes in eighteenth-century cookbooks. While strolling the perimeter of Bence Island one evening, a trading captain lost his mastiff named Ball to a crocodile, and then raced back to the fortress to avoid the same fate. Another visitor saw elephants swimming in the Sierra Leone River.

Aside from the almost cinematic good fortune of meeting Joe Opala, my research life consisted of hours in archives, trying to decipher eighteenth-century handwriting, reading old newspapers, and wondering how to build my story, which got deeper and deeper around me. I was encouraged by a verse from First Corinthians that my father had loved and always paraphrased: "For now we see through a glass, darkly, but later we shall be face to face." Dad always emphasized the *later*.

THE SLAVE TRADE'S MEN IN FULL

I John Easton of Middletown in the County of
Hartford and Colony of Connecticut, being at this time
in good Health and Sound mind and memory calling
to mind the Uncertainty of Life and the Certainty of
Death do make ordain this my last will and Testament.
. . . First, I bequeath my Soul into the Hands of its
Creator in hopes of mercy thro our Redeemer . . .

JOHN EASTON,

Wills and Codicils, Inventories

In the life of John Easton, the Middletown commander who introduced young Dudley Saltonstall to the sea, the many strands of a complex story come together. Of all the men mentioned in the logbooks, his life embodies the story of the triangle trade most completely, and his is both a success story and the reason that New England became wealthy within that first century of settlement. A descendant of one of Connecticut's earliest settlers, a deacon who had come overland from the Massachusetts Bay Colony with Thomas Hooker in 1636, Easton became a global entrepreneur centuries before the term existed, and was able to manage the triangle trade in Africa, the West Indies, and at home in New England. He was equally comfortable with the beautiful possessions of colonial gentry and the constant brutality of the slave trade.

The Connecticut River flowed past his front door. Easton, who was born in East Hartford in 1717, could walk down the stone steps of his large home and directly onto a wharf he owned. His house on the corner of Ferry Street was near the northern end of Middletown's bustling waterfront, a long curve of the Connecticut River that was home to tradesmen, mechanics, and the men who sailed brigs, snows, and sloops to the West Indies. The riverfront as drawn on an old map fairly bristled with wharves.

During the time of Easton's career in the mid-eighteenth century, Middletown was one of the largest ports in the Connecticut Colony, and its success made it a magnet for merchants and seamen. When Herman Melville's character Ishmael strolled the streets of New Bedford and wondered what had given rise to all the great mansions and park-like gardens, the answer was whaling. In John Easton's day, a century earlier, the mansions of Middletown came from a different trade—one that served a lucrative and tragic form of agriculture: the growing of sugar cane in the Caribbean by enslaved black people.

Easton spent nearly thirty years in a difficult trade that often killed the men who pursued it, so he had to have been a skilled mariner and negotiator, as well as able to keep order aboard his ships. He was also, as eighteenth-century records show, consistently employed, which meant that he was able to conduct generally profitable voyages for the men who employed him. And if John Newton's description of life aboard a slave ship is trustworthy, Easton would have had to be comfortable with the power of life and death over his crew, as well as with the tools of the trade, which included thumbscrews and whips.

Most of what can be known about John Easton's life is known because he spent his working life on the water, and there are records referencing these voyages. He sailed places. In ships carrying barrels of rum, lengths of white oak, metal tools from Europe, and iron bars, he sailed downriver from Middletown to the mouth of the Connecticut River and then to New London, a deep-water port with a waterfront on Long Island Sound. From New London, he sailed to slave trading centers along the coast of West Africa and there bought black men, women, and children and then trans-shipped them to the

opposite:

In 1836, Dr. Joseph Barratt drew a map of Main Street in Middletown as it appeared in the 1770s. His hand-drawn map, which has been recreated in type for greater legibility, shows two locations where sales of captives were held regularly: the offices of Capt. Benjamin Gleason and Dr. Thomas Walker. Map courtesy of Middlesex County Historical Society

PLAN OF MAIN STREET, MIDDLETOWN, SHOWING THE BUILDINGS AND OCCUPANTS, FROM ABOUT 1770 TO 1775.

(By JOSEPH BARRATT, M. D., Middletown, Sept. 1836.)

Easter Wetmore, *Tavern.* ▪ ▪ ------ Bassett, *Farmer.*

ROAD TO HARTFORD.

a

John Bacon, *Farmer and Constable.* ---▪ | Philip Mortimer, *Rope Maker.*

Duncan Mackintire, *Barber.* ---▪ | ------ Avenue of button wood trees.

Capt. Cotton, *Ship Master.* ---▪ | ▪---Sanford Thompson, *Ship Master.*

▪:--- Samuel Bull, *Merchant.*

Alexander Kieth, *Rope Maker.* ---▪

Philip Mortimer's *Ropewalk.* ▪ | ▪----Wait Plum, *Joiner.*
Capt. Gleason, *Slave Dealer.* ---▪ *b* | ▪--- Bezaleel Fisk, *Town Clerk.*¶
| ▪--- Capt. Ward, *Ship Master.*
Some shanties about this corner. |
WASHINGTON STREET.
'Col. Jabez Hamlin. ---▪ | ▪.--- Jacob Sebor, *Merchant.*

Joseph Wright, *Farmer.* ---▪ | ▪--- James Cornwall, *Farmer.*
Jacob Goodwin, *Sea Captain.* ---▪ |
¡Geo. Starr, *Sea Captain and Merchant.* ▪ |
| ▪--- George Phillips, *Merchant.*
Nathaniel Shalor. ---▪ | ▪--- Giles Hall, *Ship Master.*
Elisha Brewster, *Tavern Keeper.* ---▪ | ▪--- Col. Matthew Talcott, *Merchant & Farmer.*
Dr. Elliott Rawson. ---▪ |
COURT STREET.
Richard Hall, *Ship Master.* ---▪ | ▪--- Samuel Johnson, *Shoe Maker.*
| ▪--- Timothy Bigelow's *Tavern.*²*
¦John Stocken, *Iron Works.* ---▪ |
| ▪--- Joseph Southmayd, *Farmer.*
Joseph King, *Silversmith.* ---▪ | ▪--- Richard Alsop, *Merchant & Ship Owner.*
PARSONAGE STREET.
Ely, *Tanner and Shoe Maker.* ---▪ | ▪--- Capt. Doan, *Ship Master.*

Stewart, *Farmer.* ---▪ |
| ▪--- Adino Pomeroy, *Tanner.*
§John Ward. ---▪ | ▪.. Dr. Walker, *Slave Dealer.*
Ephraim Fenner, *Tavern.* ---▪ | ▪--- Capt. Thomas Goodwin.
¦Caleb Fuller. ---▪ | ▪--- William Southmayd, *Saddler.*
Timothy Boardman, *Joiner.* ---▪ |
Zac Paddock, *Joiner.* ---▪ | ▪--- Return Meigs, *Hatter.*
Elisha Clark, *Trader.* ---▪ | ▪--- Deacon Clark, *Apothecary.*
| ▪--- General Parsons.
ROAD TO NEW HAVEN. |
------ Episcopal Church.

---

* First mayor of the city, 1784.   † Built by H. Brown, a hatter.   ‡ Built by Giles Hall.
§ Built in 1678; afterwards occupied by Wensley Hobby, the first post master in the town : the post office was kept where he resided.
¦ Mr. Fuller was a schoolmaster, minister, constable, storekeeper, and kept tavern about 6 months.
¶ The office of town clerk of Middletown has been in this family 114 years.
** Gen. Washington put up at this tavern.
The letter *a*, at the head of Main street, shows the spot, or very near it, where the first meeting house was erected. *b*, town house.

British-held islands in the Caribbean, including Jamaica, Barbados, and St. Kitt's.

In the Caribbean, Easton sold most of the people he had bought in Africa, and bought molasses for the distilling of rum back home in Connecticut. He would also have brought some captive people back to the colony, for sale in New London and in Middletown, where slave *vendues* were held regularly. At the time he made his will, Easton held two Negro men, both with African names: Accrow, whose life was valued at 100 pounds, and Gambo, worth 25. They were listed in the inventory just after a meadow he owned, and just above a pair of yarn stockings.

Though he was a confirmed "Guinea trader," as Africa-bound commanders were often called, there is evidence that Easton also made several whaling voyages, because he appears in an account book of Middletown sea captain and merchant Samuel Willis settling debts "by cash rec'd of him on whaling voyage" and by "his part of whale boats." Colonists began whale fishing almost the moment they arrived, and Easton's whaling voyages were probably made in Long Island Sound.

To serve as commander of a slave ship seemed to have required a certain severity of nature, and a particular set of skills as well as maritime know-how and the ability to command. In addition to the extraordinary hardships of life on board an eighteenth-century vessel, slaving vessels faced the circumstance of an unhappy human cargo that wanted, very legitimately, to reverse what was happening to them and to escape by any means necessary.

Even in Saltonstall's brief narrative, there is an account of an uprising, though not on Easton's ship. New England newspapers of the era are full of captives attacking their captors, and Easton would have had to keep constant watch against that, particularly when his ships were near the African coast and a slave could hold at least a slim hope of fleeing successfully.

Easton also made the voyage directly from Connecticut to the Caribbean islands, ferrying horses, livestock such as chickens and pigs, and food. (One line in Easton's 1770 will and inventory lists "746 swine.") The onions, potatoes, and other Connecticut-grown crops were to feed the enslaved people growing sugar on the islands, and the Connecticut-grown horses were to plow the cane fields and turn the wheels in the fiery sugar mills where the cane was crushed and refined into cane juice, which was eventually crystallized into sugar. For its brutality, constant danger, and suffering forced on its captive workers, scholar Adam Hochschild has described this agricultural system as "deadly" and "one of the hardest ways of life on earth."

Yet for Easton and the men whose names appear with his in the customs records, account books, and newspapers, the lethal nature of growing sugar cane was part of the equation for success. Over the past half century, as scholars have tried to come to terms with the baseline economics of New World enslavement, it has become clearer that despite a competitive market that caused the price of slaves purchased in West Africa to increase, it was still cheaper to buy a human being there than to raise one to working age in the Caribbean.

David Brion Davis, an important scholar of the slave trade and the first to delineate the crucial difference between slavery in ancient cultures and the system of hereditary slavery that took root in the Caribbean and the New World, writes that the price for a captive increased 400 percent between about 1680 and 1780, yet it was still cheaper to import a person in Africa than to raise one from birth. And Davis adds another cost to the human equation: "The assumption that Africans were somehow 'hardier' necessarily omits the unrecorded death tolls from place of capture or initial sale even to the African coast. Planters could disregard such losses unless the cumulative costs inflated the price of slaves to a prohibitive level."

The monetization of black lives held as slaves was straightforward, and Easton would have understood its terrible arithmetic perfectly. The problem for slave traders was not that sugar agriculture killed and disabled its workers, nor that the crushing nature of the labor reduced the fertility of the female captives; the problem was keeping the plantations supplied with fresh workers. For a savvy officer and slave trader like Easton, the plantation system of the West Indies was not a business built on suffering, but one of nearly endless opportunity.

Irishman Nicholas Owen met Easton in Africa and sailed with him briefly in 1756 but did not like him, and said that unless the conversation was about farming or slave trading, "which he was very good at," Easton grew impatient. That same year, Easton captained Gurdon Saltonstall's snow *Fox* to Sierra Leone, where he purchased 109 captives. Owen very likely assisted Easton with his trading at that time, and in July 1756 Easton landed 90 captives in Annapolis, Maryland.

Nicholas Owen was an independent white trader working on the coast of Sierra Leone for most of the years between 1746 and 1759, when he died after months of a debilitating fever. Reading his vivid, complaint-filled journal, which was not published until 1930, is like being handed a snapshot from the past. A small-scale trader in slaves, camwood, ivory, and other commodities, Owen was probably typical of the many independent white traders who worked on that stretch of coast—able to scratch together enough to build a small house and sustain an African wife, but not successful enough to leave Africa and return to Europe to live in the "granduour" that had once described his family's fortune. Where Saltonstall's logs offer telegraphic information on the passage of each day, Owen's *Journal of a Slave-Dealer*, which covers the same trade and stretch of coast as the logbooks, is richly detailed and cranky.

Owen wrote,

> It was common after company was broke up and every man at quarters that Capt. Easton began his discourse conserning the absent company in the most ungenerous terms, as Mr.-Such-a-one was deeply indebted, or another's wife was under suspision of takeing an opertunity while her husband was tradeing in the country, occasioned him to be noted amongst all his acquinatance in Africa. He had good officers and commonly made good voy-

ages for his merchants, which might be the occasion of his preferment at home.

I wondered what Saltonstall, who was the descendant of colonial aristocrats and governors, thought of his captain, of whom Owen also remarked that he lacked "good breeding." Saltonstall's name carried the colonial era cachet of a Kennedy or a Rockefeller, and seeing that he sailed aboard ships his father owned, he may not have been hand selected by Easton as his first mate.

"It has been seldom known such a scarcety of shiping upon this coast as at the present time and such a bad time of trade," Owen wrote in the spring of 1757, "from Siera Lone to Cape Mount there [is] not above 3 or 4 ships of sail that come for trade, which is of bad consequence to us that lives in the country."

In her introduction to the 1930 edition of Owen's *Journal*, scholar Eveline Martin notes that while an escalating demand for African labor on plantations in the Caribbean and the American colonies solidified English and colonial involvement in the trade, it remained a complex endeavor. It was, she writes, "not a simple matter of deporting the population of sea-coast regions, but a most elaborate and efficiently organized trade, dependent upon the works of various groups of African middlemen in the interior." A fortress like the one on Bence Island, or Cape Coast Castle—where Easton and Saltonstall also traded—was the last and most visible piece of an extended network of trade.

Over the course of two centuries, an estimated 3 million Africans were carried to islands in the Caribbean to grow sugar. At the time of emancipation there in 1834, the census of the enslaved showed less than 700,000 because 200 years of harsh labor, malnutrition, disease, and suffering had caused the population to dwindle rather than increase. Adam Hochschild points out that growing and milling sugar cane was a form of agriculture so harsh, so lethal, and so destructive to the health of its captive workers that by the middle of the eighteenth century, only one-half of the women bore children. This number contrasts compellingly with that of the American colonies. Though American slavery was never benign and was also a system governed by oppression, fear, and violence, the approximately 400,000 captives brought to colonial America numbered, by the time of emancipation in the Caribbean, nearly 2 million, with 319,000 African Americans living in freedom.

John Easton was a charter member in 1754 of St. John's Lodge of Free and Accepted Masons in Middletown. Named the lodge's first secretary, Easton and his fellow Masons met at the centrally located home and tavern of Captain Michael Burnham, who had recently resettled from Hartford to Middletown and was also involved in the West Indies trade.

Burnham's life illuminates the dangers of the West Indies trade that Easton escaped. In 2011, Michael Burnham's grave was discovered in Suriname, on the northern coast of South America, along with the eighteenth-century graves of three other ships' captains, two from Rhode Island and one from New London. Burnham, who is buried under a stone carved with the head of an angel in a Dutch colonial cemetery in Paramaribo, the capital, may have been protecting local interests in Suriname, where slaves grew sugar cane, coffee, cocoa, and cotton in a plantation system that was particularly infamous for its cruelty. The *New-London Summary* noted that Burnham "was a Gentleman greatly beloved and his Death is as much lamented." (William Blake's famous and horrific engravings of tortured slaves were based on soldier John Stedman's account of Suriname in the 1770s. Stedman, who was in Dutch Suriname for five years to help quell a series of uprisings by the enslaved, said in his narrative that "the clang of the whip" and the screams of the slaves went "from morning till night." Though not an abolitionist, Stedman said that the horrors he witnessed made him physically ill.)

At the foot of Ferry Street where John Easton's house once stood, you can look across a narrow stretch of river to an edging of trees, a few low commercial buildings, and a boatyard. Low-income housing built in 2010 now stands on the site of Easton's house. The house was torn

Commander and slave trader John Easton built this house in Middletown on the Connecticut River in about 1750, and filled it with the beautiful possessions of a successful mid-eighteenth-century sea captain. By the time it was torn down in 1949, it no longer resembled the property Easton had assembled with outbuildings, enclosures for animals, and a wharf on the river. Photograph courtesy of Middlesex County Historical Society

down in 1949 because it stood on what would become a new road along the river, and although the year of its construction is not known, records show that Easton purchased the land in 1746. He lived there with his wife, Sarah Ward Easton, from the time they built their house until her death in 1768. Easton apparently did not remarry, and lived there until his death in 1774—from an illness described in the *New-London Gazette* as "short but painful"—and bequeathed the house and "all the appurtenances therein to belong" to his nephew John Stocking Chauncey, the son of his sister Mary. Easton was fifty-seven when he died.

The center-chimney house had beams that were hand hewn with a broad ax, and was pegged with wooden pins. The foundations and the chimney were made of fieldstone, and the back of the house had a sloping, saltbox shape. By the time the house was torn down, porches and exterior stairways had been added, and the "Magill place," as it was called, was home to several families and directly adjacent to train tracks and a railroad crossing.

John Easton traveled tens of thousands of nautical miles during his thirty-five years at sea, but he is buried just a short walk from where his riverfront home once stood. Philip Mortimer, who had also been involved in the shipping trades of the eighteenth century, donated the land on which he had owned a ropewalk just a block from the Connecticut River. Middletown was settled in 1650, and Mortimer Cemetery is the third oldest of the city's twenty-four cemeteries. Its ancient stones fill a city block in a neighborhood that is poor, and the cemetery's massive iron gates are held closed with a length of rusted chain and a scarred padlock. The padlock key hangs on a nail at the Main Street firehouse around the corner, so I retrieved it for my visit.

I couldn't make the key work in the lock on the bitter February day when I first visited, so I decided to return on a milder day. It was August before I got back to search for Easton's grave, and after unsuccessfully trying the key again on what was once the main entrance to the cemetery, I found a much smaller gate, hidden by a health food store and a parked car. The key worked perfectly, and I leaned on the gate, which creaked open like the gate in a ghost story.

I had read that Easton was buried under a table stone, which was then considered a mark of status, but the table stones I found, waist-high slabs of marble supported by carved columns, were indecipherable after centuries of exposure. On upright headstones made from red sandstone and brownstone, I saw the surnames of men and women Easton would have known: Southmayd, Magill—trader Arthur Magill bought Easton's house after his death—Wetmore and Sage, Bacon and Southworth. I began to think I might not find Easton's grave because many of the stones are deeply eroded by age, and the low iron barriers that families used to mark their plots have been knocked over or fallen down.

I had walked toward a tree for a moment's shade from the sun when I looked down and saw a large, table-style stone lying on the grass. Carved from red sandstone, it was the grave of Captain Philip Mortimer, the donor of the cemetery land and the largest slaveholder in Middletown. Around the edges of the massive flat stone—which is the size of about three conventional headstones of the era—other names are carved, along with their death dates, and one of them is for "Capt. John Easton." At the top of the large stone, the word "Friends" is carved with a flourish, and beneath that word is a four-line prayer asking the living to leave these bones in peace and permit them to settle into dust.

I had thought the cemetery would be arranged by the ages of the stones, with the oldest graves all in one place. But the families of the dead must have walked this grass over the centuries and then simply chosen the place that appealed to them. From Easton's edge of Captain Mortimer's stone, you can see eighteenth-century gravestones with winged faces, the Egyptian obelisks of nineteenth-century businessmen, an American flag hung with a wreath for veterans, and a Victorian marble plinth bearing the sculpture of a woman, weeping.

When I returned the key to a burly fireman at the station, he asked, "Find what you were looking for?"

I explained that I had found the grave of an eighteenth-century slave ship captain, a character in a book I was writing. It would have been truer to say that I didn't know what I was looking for. I don't know why I am called to the ground where the men in the logbooks lived and died, or why I search for examples of their handwriting, and study the old maps showing their destinations and the harbors they sailed from. I know that I am trying to persuade myself that a history that seems utterly implausible really did occur, and that the story I want to tell is real.

John Easton was part of a trade system that dehumanized black people from the moment it encountered them. He traded for them in a place that was utterly foreign to the colonial Connecticut he knew, then he stowed them aboard ships like firewood or furniture—which do not have feelings—and then took them to Caribbean islands and sold them as he also sold livestock. From this exchange, he realized sufficient profit to create a substantial homestead and estate. In all this, which would have taken months, he could not allow fellow feeling or pity or curiosity or tenderness.

And although he would have seen these black people weep and rage, sweat and suffer, eat and drink, they never became real enough to him for him to say, "I can't do this." Like the English captain John Newton, who referred to his captives by the numerical order in which he acquired them, as when he noted on January 31, 1753, "Buryed a slave girl (No. 92)," to Easton they were not human.

Slavery was not new in the colonies when Easton made his voyages, and it endured for more than a century after them. The habit of *not* feeling around these people would already have been deep by Easton's lifetime. Did our refusal to acknowledge their humanness doom us, from the first moment of making a person captive on American soil, to become an unequal society? The empathic failure that allowed the colonies to become a nation with slaves was a socioeconomic decision that was, and is, a human catastrophe.

Despite its centrality to the American story, slavery continues to be defined narrowly, as if, for instance, the great-granddaughter of nineteenth-century white immigrants does not have as legitimate a relationship with the injustice at our nation's core as the descendants of the enslaved. Slavery is not limited to the body of the captive and the estate of the owner, but encompasses those who served the slave trade, made its engines, profited from its wealth, and countenanced its existence. It encompasses those of us who followed the generations of enslavement, and if we celebrate the brave deeds and proud accomplishments of our ancestors as part of what it means to be an American, we must also accommodate, as part of our national story, the profound human failure that permitted slavery.

This history of slavery has not ended, and its damage is alive in the present. I think of the angel of history as described by Walter Benjamin, the German philosopher who committed suicide while trying to escape the Nazis in 1940. Benjamin's angel turns his face toward the past, and where we see a chain of human events that can be explained, he sees a single catastrophe, which hurls wreckage upon wreckage at his feet. The angel wants to awaken the dead, Benjamin writes, and make whole what was smashed, but a powerful storm is blowing in with a wind so violent the angel cannot close his wings.

...le Imployd abo rugging Carp. & joiner making awnin...
...r Making a Pump Can ⸺ No Trade at all ⸺

...rday July 15th 1758 this 24 hours Light Winds & pleas. ...
...Imployd overhawling Blocks Carp.rs & joiner Making ...
...ng ⸺ No Trade only Bought Some Corn & planting ...

...ay July 16th this 24 hours Light Winds & pleas. Wear. Peop...
...yd abo. Jobs Carp.r & joiner abo. the awning the Cap. o...
...Wanton Purchased one boy Slave of Quaquo...

...day July 17. this 24 hours Light Winds & pleas. Wear. Peo...
...oyd over hawling tobacco Carp.r & joiner abo. the awning ...
...rade at all ⸺ Saild for Sirrenam the Large Dutch ...
...500 & od Slaves on board ⸺

...ay July 18. this 24 hours Light Winds & pleas. Wear. Peop...
...y in yr Hold & fetching Brazeal Tobacco from a Dute...
...Cap.t Buley ⸺ Purchased one man Slave ⸺

...esday July 19. this 24 hours Light Winds but a Large s...
...le Imployd picking Tobacco No Trade at all ⸺

...day July 20. this 24 hours Calm & little wind People Imployd...
...Hold Cooper a Cutting Rum Hhd Purchased Two Slave...
...essely in yr Rhode Except Three Poor Rum Men ⸺
...d the yaul up to Clean ⸺ broacht a bl Bee...

...y July 20 this 24 hours Calm Weather People Imployd ove...
...old & found a Hogs. No 86 Leaked all out No 85 only 54 Gal. in ...
...gin to yr Cap.t ⸺ Leakage ocationed by all yr Head Hoops fly...
...rade this 24 hours ⸺ the agreed with my Lord to Send a man...
...to accraw after yr Longboat for 4 Gal.s Trade Rum ⸺

...rday July 21.st this 24 hours Calm Wear. People Imployd fil...
...head with Water & with Rum Cooper a Cutting Hogs...
...d from yr Longboat by a Letter from Underwood w...
...at Mumford with 3 Slaves on board ⸺

...day July 22.d this 24 hours Calm & hazey Weather at 10 ...
...ye Ship to W. Ward which we Suppos'd to be the English Man of ...

FIVE

Separations

A VISIT TO MADINA

Pray I will and sing I must,
And yet I weep . . .
WILLIAM BUTLER YEATS

Once, *Bence* had been simply a mysterious word on a document printed out from a microfilm machine, a place I could not imagine and that I didn't know would summon me.

After Britain outlawed the slave trade in 1807, the traffic in human beings continued, illegally, for decades, often with New Englanders at the helm. But the law did end slave trading at Bence Island.

The same geography that had made the island a success as a slaving center and brought the ships of Europe and the New World to its tiny shore to buy captives was also its undoing. British vessels were anchored in Freetown Harbor, which slaving ships had to cross before heading upriver to Bence Island, and this de facto blockage had a chilling effect on the once-thriving fortress. When Great Britain took up arms against the slave trade it had captained for centuries, its interdiction of slaving vessels was vigorous.

The rivers that had once ferried slaves from the interior down to Bence were used until the 1830s to move logs to a sawmill on the island,

After a Sierra Leonean physician named M. C. F. Easmon helped bring the history of Bence Island back into view in the late 1940s, this model of the fortress itself—which was much more intact then than today—was made. It is on display in the Sierra Leone National Museum in Freetown. Courtesy of Tom Brown/ *Hartford Courant*

and though the trading in slaves continued in the area, Bence Island was too well known and too easy to police.

In the Sierra Leone National Museum in Freetown, I studied a plaster model of Bence Island made after the island's rediscovery in 1947 by a medical doctor named M. C. F. Easmon. A Sierra Leonean who believed in preserving local history, Dr. Easmon and a team visited Bence and uncovered ruins encased by more than a century of vines and vegetation. In his notes, which are held in the national museum, Easmon wrote, "Nothing of the ruins could be seen from the river and the way had to be hacked through to them. The general clearing of the undergrowth took place, leaving numerous large trees in front of[,] around and growing on the numerous walls." He and his team found tall, mature trees growing up in the very center of the enclosures where slaves had been held. He memorably described the island as the place "where history sleeps," and was instrumental in its being named a national historic landmark in 1948.

The plaster model shows parts of the ruins that have collapsed in the past sixty-five years, including a guardroom and the upper floor of Bance Island House, but it perfectly captures the darkness of the place. The museum, a smallish bungalow-style building that once housed a telephone exchange, has an impressive name but few resources, and its collections seem more random than complete: models of the *Amistad*, hundreds of carvings, children's school projects, shards of Chinese porcelain from a shipwreck discovered in 1974, a valuable Fresnel beacon from a lighthouse, and worn maps.

Amid the ceremonial masks, straw baskets, and smooth carvings of stone, ivory, and wood, the model of Bence Island is jarring and ominous. The model shows the ruins of the fortress completed in 1796, a place built at the direction of the last English owners, and is a powerful reminder of the commerce Europeans brought to Africa. The carvings, some of them small enough to fit into the palm of one's hand, feel deeply local. With their representations of gods and creatures who were loved or feared, they open a world distinctly linked to this place. The castle, with its spaces for guards and gunpowder, slaves and traders, suggests a system and a horror brought from a different world.

When the slave trade at Bence Island ended, many of the grommetos who had assisted in the slave trade moved further upriver past Bence, and established a village that today is called Madina. They returned to making their livelihood from fishing and growing rice. Over the long decades of the slave trade, these free black workers had lived in their own communities on the islands of the archipelago. One of their villages on Bence was named for their chief, Adam, and his impressive gravestone is just a few steps from the grove where white company agents and mariners are buried.

The grommetos, who were paid and protected from enslavement along with their wives and children, were part of Bence's success story.

In a climate that was lethal to white people with no immunity to yellow fever, malaria, and other tropical diseases, grommetos performed the essential labor of caring for the slaves and guarding them, as well as growing food for the fortress itself and making repairs to visiting ships. They also managed and tended the company's "out-factories," which were holding areas on other islands and along the coast where captives were gathered for later sale at Bence. Company ships also scoured the coast to trade for slaves, and grommetos were often at the helm. They were, to use a modern term, the support system for the European slave warehouses, and the decision of Richard Oswald's company to "Africanize" its operations on and around Bence Island was the key to its great success.

Grommetos were not despised by their neighbors, nor was their prestige harmed by their involvement in the trade. Joe Opala, who has studied the slave trade on the Sierra Leone River for more than thirty years, believes that the slave trade introduced a system of brutality that, in the long run, could not be resisted.

Madina is not on any map, but I wanted to meet the descendants of the black workers who had once lived on Bence, so after our first visit to the island, we met Madina's chief, a slender, distinguished man who sometimes carries an umbrella as his badge of office, and he agreed that we could come for a visit to his community. Bai Adam Foday Kabbah is the direct descendant of the revered Bai, or chief, Adam of two centuries ago, after whom generations of chiefs have been named. He met us at Bence, and we watched as he performed a ceremony of reverence at his ancestor's grave.

After just a few days in Sierra Leone, I was already knee-deep in the complexities of the slave trade. For what seem like the most human of reasons—to protect themselves from enslavement and for gain—many of the region's Temne people had been willing participants in the trade. To Tasso Island, which had been fully involved in the slave trading enterprise on Bence, I had brought a copy of the ship's log and given it to the chief of Sangbulima village. Ancient and blind, he was

From the archives of the Connecticut State Library in Hartford, I brought a copy
of the logbooks to Alimamy Rakka, chief of Sangbulima village on Tasso Island.
During the years of the slave trade, Tasso supported the fortress on Bence Island.
The whole community in the chief's village gathered for the ceremony. Courtesy
of Tom Brown/*Hartford Courant*

surrounded by the members of his village as I gave him the photo-
copied pages and apologized for my country's role in slavery and in the
damage to his ancestors. Because I was in Africa before doing much of
my research, only later did I learn that Alimamy Rakka, the gracious
chief who had made me welcome in his village, was probably the descendant of island people who assisted in the trade at Bence.

Madina village felt like a long way from anywhere, though it is
only about seven miles upriver past Bence. The dense green river-
banks showed no sign of other villages or commerce, and this section
of the Sierra Leone River felt particularly remote and haunted. For
more than a century, slaves were carried down this river to Bence,
sometimes arriving at the island with their skin scraped bloody and
raw from the rough wood of the carved dugout "canoos."

On a high tide, our deft little motorboat made it partway to Madina, but then even its shallow draft was too much, and we climbed down into Morlai Bangura's small wooden boat. Two at a time, we made the rest of the journey through mangrove swamp and rice fields. In places, the vegetation closed over our heads, and we seemed to be moving through an airless green tunnel of tall rice plants.

I had read accounts of the crocodiles in the Sierra Leone River and its tributaries—all the eighteenth-century visitors' accounts include extremely accurate drawings of crocodiles, jaws bristling with sharp teeth—and I had noticed that even today, people heft a good-sized piece of log into the river to test for the nearness of crocodiles before wading in.

Even with just three passengers, Bangura's little skiff tipped alarmingly, and my hands, clenched on the boat gunnels, were just inches above the water. Joe Opala, seated in front of me, said that I shouldn't worry, because the local people are such good boatmen they never learn to swim. The afternoon shaded into a greenish gray, typical of late day in this region just before rain, and Bangura turned the boat a little to the right. A long field of mud dotted with pools of water opened in front of us.

On the other side of the field, a group of people from Madina were waiting. Dressed in the long robes of observant Muslims, they stood motionless in the fading light. They looked as if they had been there forever.

On the shore in deeper shade, three maroon lawn chairs, the cheap plastic kind you usually see in white, stacked outside big-box stores, had been set up for us. A man wearing a baseball cap took my hand as I stepped from the boat onto the mud. I slipped but he steadied me, saying, "Ah, Madam," and led me across the wet ground, which was damp and smelled like earth and swamp. A queenly woman in her seventies, wearing an ankle-length dress and matching turban of sea-green silk, placed a few leaves on a rock, as if to soften the seat, and then sat down when I sat. I was sunburned and disheveled, and felt ashamed of my dirty clothes.

(Before our visit to Sierra Leone, I had made arrangements to rent a house for us in Freetown, one with a small kitchen and a washing machine, but a man with a connection to the property had stolen our rent money and disappeared. By the time I got to Freetown, our house man was cooking over a fire in the side yard, no one had been paid, there was neither electricity nor hot water in the house, and a man with a machine gun seemed to have made himself at home. We moved to a modest hotel for the rest of our stay, and each evening I would swish around in the cracked bathtub one of the two outfits I had brought to Africa.)

People smiled at me, but no one spoke. It was Ramadan, and they would not break their fast for several hours. In the lengthening and comfortable silence, as we waited for the boatman to ferry my colleagues up from the boat, I thought, *This is as far from home as I will ever get.* I had wanted to enter, in as physical a way as I could, the story of human enslavement so that I could try to understand it. That longing had brought me to what felt like the edge of the world.

We walked a mile through the jungle, the heavy canopy of trees making the forest like a windowless room at twilight. We paused at the graves of earlier chiefs, and stopped to acknowledge each one. For a moment, I thought the graves had been cleared for us to see them better, then realized that these graves are always kept clear and clean, as an act of reverence.

Arriving at Madina, we were each handed a kola nut, a traditional West African symbol of welcome. Kola nuts are very hard, and these had been soaking in a bucket of water to soften. The fruit of an evergreen tree that is native to tropical rain forests, the kola nut tastes bitter at first, but then sweetens in the mouth.

A small goat the color of smoke was tethered to a post in the large thatched-roof house where we gathered for the ceremony. Several days earlier, I had given the chief money for the goat so that it could be sacrificed for a community feast. The goat had long eyelashes and that Mona Lisa half-smile you see on lambs; during a long interval of prayers, the little goat looked around equably, and then was led to a corner out of our view and killed with a long knife by the community's imam.

The village felt small, and more cloistered than Tasso Island's Sangbulima village, where we had been entertained with music and dancing and a stilt walker so skilled he could climb trees in his wooden stilts. At Madina, the children sang for us, and I distributed Walmart watches to the chief and subchiefs, but the mood was solemn and prayerful. The village imam was a tall, almost emaciated man whose skin was an ashen black, and at one point during the prayers, he lifted his face from his hands to glare at the children, who were giggling at the white strangers.

Madina has neither electricity nor running water, and its houses are built of cement blocks and thatch. There are no screens in the windows, and everywhere the floors are simply earth, swept clean. The pathways within the village also are swept clean, but in terms of material things, the people own very little.

I sat with Bai Adam Foday Kabbah on a small porch sheltered from the rain, and asked if he felt sorrow or regret about his long-ago ancestors' participation in the slave trade. Through a translator, Bai Adam said that the descendants of slaves in America have much more than he and the people of his village have. The people sold into slavery were criminals and victims of war, he said, echoing an explanation that I had often heard and did not believe. His eyes slid away from me. He was angry with me, and despite the gift of the goat and the inexpensive watch, which he spun around and around on his bone-thin wrist, my questions probably seemed rude. Rude and irrelevant. He honors his ancestors each time he passes their graves, and wants to build a school for the children of the village. Why am I asking about guilt?

Bai Adam said that his people had done what they had to do to survive.

We walked back toward the boat, this time across a narrow dirt path rapidly turning to mud in the heavy rain. It was hard walking because a man from the village was trying to hold an umbrella over my head, and a tiny girl named Zainab walked close to me, holding my hand. She wore a string of navy-blue beads around her slender wrist, and had beads woven into each of her many braids.

When I looked back at her from the boat, I saw, through a scrim of rain, that she had lifted both hands and was waving goodbye.

THIS FAR, AND NO FURTHER

In early October of 2007, my mother began to die.

Three months earlier, Chas and Kate and I had moved her from the dementia wing of an assisted-living residence near us to a facility about thirty minutes away. This new place specialized in the care of people with dementia, and my sister worked there as director of communications and development. Mama went from a low-tech cocoon to a place that was designed to engage her, and to better address her lengthening list of frailties.

But Mama was done. She was eighty-four, and had end-stage arthritis in her knees, which made walking witheringly painful. Even turning in her little bed caused her to gasp with pain. Her mother, who had bequeathed this malady to her, had pronounced it *arthuritis*, like the man's name. We had tried different medications over the years, but the only one that worked came with a long list of possible side effects including damage to the stomach lining, and ulcers.

At her new residence one Sunday morning, my mother pushed her pancakes listlessly around the plate. I moved my chair closer to hers, and put my arm around her. "Not hungry, Mama?" I whispered. The television that looped endlessly through old movies and early sitcoms was on in the next room, the recorded laughter braying, and the aides were beginning to clear away the remains of breakfast, gently clinking the silverware against the plates.

I knew that Mama didn't understand where she was, or what was happening to her. Bewilderment had come to engulf her, every hour of the day. She could not read, could barely walk, and though she did not spout harsh gibberish and nonsense words like some of the other residents, she did not really talk anymore.

Mama and I turned toward each other so that she could rest her head on my shoulder. She took that first deep breath that precedes weeping, and began to cry. The aides quietly removed the last of the dishes and left us alone in the dining room. Mama barely made a sound, but I could feel her tears wet the front of my shirt. Her head was tucked under my chin, and she relaxed against me as I held her wrecked life in my arms.

Seven years earlier, a few weeks before he collapsed and died, my father had given me his death notice, which he had written himself. "I know that I'm not going to get well," he said, "and I would like to have this in the newspaper after I die. I thought you could take care of this for me." He told me that I should feel free to add anything I wanted. He was calm, and wanted to talk about his career. In his death notice, he had listed only a few of his awards because he believed that most of the prizes handed out in the federal service were, to use his word, spurious. He laughed when I told him that death notices were free for the families of staffers at the newspaper—I knew he would think that was mordantly funny—and before I left, he held me for a long moment, then said, "Good girl."

As I held my silent mother, I remembered the book of poems I'd found on Dad's night table the week after his death. The poems were written by Stanley Kunitz late in his life, and a neat slice of Kleenex, Dad's preferred bookmark, was tucked into the poem he had read last. "Who knows, when the time comes to say goodbye, / what separation we are meant to bear . . ."

I hadn't imagined that moment with Dad at the dining room table, his yellowing citations spread around him and the neatly typed death notice, nor had I imagined sitting with my weeping mother at the empty breakfast table. They were my parents, my history. I expected them to get old and frail, but not, actually, to die.

A week later, my mother began to vomit blood. The medication that had relieved her pain for so long had also done what it threatened it might do and worn holes in the walls of her stomach. In the corridor of a nearby hospital later that day, a doctor outlined what the remedies might be, and said that she had been very brave during the painful examination she had undergone. When my sister and I went into her room, Mama was whispering to herself, incoherently, and saying over and over that she was sorry, that she wouldn't do it again. "Holy shit," Kate muttered. "This is bad." Mother thought she was being punished for something she had done, and was apologizing to her own punishing mother, who had found her unlovable as a child, a burden, and belittled her even in adulthood.

Three weeks later, after the return to her residence, a final break with reality, escalating pain, and many consultations with the medical staff, Mama lay in a hospice unit, sedated with morphine and floating toward her death. I sat by her for several days, as did my brother Chas and his wife. My sister popped in every hour, neat in her business suits and jewelry. When Kate could stay, we'd stroke Mama's hands and feet and murmur to her in the low soft voice she had used with us, as children.

When Kate and I were small, we had invented a bedtime game in which we were brave state troopers named Clay and Morgan. We communicated over our pretend walkie-talkies about a dangerous and deranged criminal named the Peanut Lady, who was "holed up" in a cabin in the hills. Actually, the Peanut Lady was just Mama, having her bath on Saturday night and enjoying a rare half hour of solitude.

As we stood by her bed now, Kate smoothed our mother's hair back from her forehead and whispered, "Come out with your hands up. We know you're in there."

Unconscious, all pain and anxiety erased by the morphine that was slowing her heart, my mother was beautiful again. Her skin seemed at times to glow. I forgave her for preferring my sister to me, and for her occasional coldness toward me when I was a teenager. I asked her forgiveness for the worry and disappointment I knew I had caused, and told her, over and over, that my love was strong around her.

I was about to head home late one afternoon when a volunteer who came in each day to sing to the residents entered Mama's room. "Oh my," she said, looking at my mother. "You had better get your sister."

Though Mama was breathing very calmly, there began to be long spaces between each breath. For about twenty minutes, my sister and I had our arms around her, our own breathing almost suspended during the lengthening pauses. She took a last long breath and then did not draw another. "Oh mum," my sister said, her voice thick with tenderness and grief. A nurse in green scrubs stepped to the bedside and placed his stethoscope against Mama's heart. I asked him if she was dead, and he said gently, looking more at her than me, "She is."

We touched Mama's face, stroked her hair, and kissed her. Kate and I held each other, and then she left to be with close friends. I called Chas, and then sat with Mama for an hour while papers were signed and the funeral home contacted. Her room had been kept dimly lit, and it got darker as the daylight faded. The rain made a steady sigh against the window, and from my mother, there was, forever, no sound at all.

LEGACY

During our time on Bence Island, on an eroding slope of earth below the fortress and not far from the barracoon where slaves had been held for sale, Joseph Opala found human remains. In his three decades of studying the island, Joe said, he had found every kind of eighteenth-century remnant, including a carved seal of office from Napoleonic France, but this was the first time he had found bone from a human being.

While walking on the shore, Joe saw two small teeth emerging from the ground. Brushing gently at the loose soil surrounding them, he saw that the teeth were set into a piece of jawbone and knew at once that it was the jawbone of a child.

The half-buried fragment of lower jaw was small and narrow, and some of its teeth had not fully developed. The forensic examiner in Freetown thought the bone might be ten or fifteen years old, perhaps from a child whose family had hidden on Bence during Sierra Leone's long civil war, which had raged throughout the 1990s. During that decade, people had sought shelter wherever they could from the chaos and slaughter. Neighboring Tasso Island, whose three villages have a combined population of about 700, had nearly 5,000 people living on the island during one point in the conflict. That number had so overtaxed the resources of the island, which has neither running water nor electricity, that cholera—an enteric disease that comes from drinking contaminated water—broke out.

But the jawbone fragment, which is discolored and resembles stone or driftwood more than bone, looked old to Joe. At the request of the Sierra Leone National Museum and with the permission of the national government, he brought it to the United States, where it was examined by Andrew Hill, a professor of anthropology at Yale University and head of the anthropology division at the Peabody Museum of Natural History in New Haven. Hill, who usually studies fossil remains from prehistory, said the fragment was at least two or three centuries old. I showed a photograph of the bone to my dentist, and he pulled down his mask to study it. "A six-year-old," he said softly.

When Joe went to collect the fragment from the Peabody Museum before shipping it to the University of South Carolina for further study, I went with him, and held the bone in my hand. The piece of jawbone holds four teeth, molars.

The bone weighed nothing in my hand, and still smelled, faintly, of earth.

I spent days looking for examples of his handwriting. In the eighteenth century, nearly everything was written by hand, so I thought that among the many papers and documents of Dudley Saltonstall's famous family, I would come across something that was signed or written by him that would be stunningly like the handwriting in the ships' logbooks.

On this score, however, I had already been stunningly—and very publicly—wrong. For the long newspaper article I had written on the logbooks, I made a tentative identification of the logbook keeper as Samuel Gould, the son of a farmer from eastern Connecticut who had a lot of children and not enough land to divide among them. The words "Sam Gould" were written on the logbooks' inside cover, just where a person would jot his name if the book were his. For a man to be the supercargo or chief mate aboard a ship in the mid-eighteenth century, he would have been youngish, probably less than twenty-five. In the colonial birth records of the 1720s, 1730s, and early 1740s, there weren't a lot of candidates who could have been my Sam, but there was one. At the time of the logbooks, Killingly, where farmer Gould had lived, had been part of New London County, and Gould had had, among his large family, two sons close in age—a Samuel and a Thomas.

At that time in colonial America, spelling was often phonetic, and Gould, Gold, and Goold were spelled so interchangeably that two of the three names sometimes appear on the same records. At the Connecticut State Library, I searched through wills and probate records, looking for Goulds. In the will of a Samuel Gould who died in Fairfield in 1769, the handwriting was eerily similar to the handwriting in the logbooks. This Gould had left to his wife a black child named Lively.

If this were the Sam of the logbooks, it would have meant that he didn't grow old, but the man who kept the logbooks mentions having "fitts," one so severe that he dislocated his jaw, and he mentions going to see a doctor in St. Kitts. But I knew that I badly wanted to close the case on the identification of the log keeper, and I also knew that my eagerness—and ego—made my judgment suspect.

A handwriting expert in Rhode Island examined pages from the logbooks, pages from the Fairfield will, and several other eighteenth-century Connecticut wills involving Goulds. He identified some distinctive similarities between the Fairfield will and the logbooks, but also noted that penmanship was highly conforming at that time.

But the tentative identification of Samuel Gould as the author of the logbooks didn't look very tentative once it was published in the newspaper project I wrote about the logbooks. Later, I puzzled over the odds that a genealogist and direct descendant of the Fairfield Samuel Gould would be living in Connecticut and interested enough to wade through my thirty-six-page Sunday supplement on the logbooks. Those unlikely odds turned out to be much better than I had imagined. The Fairfield Gould, as the genealogist's evidence showed, was old at the time of his death. And yes, he was a slave owner, and there was slave ownership in the family, but he could not have been the same man who wrote the logbooks. She requested, and I wrote, a lengthy retraction.

I kept studying the logbooks and looking for connections. At the same time that the Connecticut State Library had purchased the logbooks from the widow of a collector, the library had acquired from her a notebook of provisions that were taken aboard the frigate *Trumbull*, which had been provisioned out of New London in 1777.

One of thirteen ships commissioned by the Continental Congress, the *Trumbull* was a twenty-four-gun frigate, built in a Connecticut River shipyard about twenty-six miles from New London and launched in 1776. Listed among the crew was a Nathan Gould, which gave a little more weight to the possibility that the logbooks were maintained by a Gould. Perhaps the two documents had been fellow travelers over time, connected to a family named Gould and never separated. I asked a research librarian how likely that was, and he said only, "Possible."

As it turned out, I had the right church but the wrong pew. When I had first studied the provisioning records for the *Trumbull,* I had noticed that there was milk provided for the officers, but not the name of the commanding officer: Dudley Saltonstall. I didn't know, then, that he was the most likely keeper of the logbooks, and that his father had owned two of the ships and helped underwrite the voyages, nor did I know that the sailing orders for the third voyage showed Dudley as second in command aboard the *Fox.* My fellow travelers had been, most probably, not in the Gould family, but among the Saltonstalls.

I had looked far and wide when I should just have looked closely. I knew that Dudley's father Gurdon was the deputy, or mayor, of New London, and that Gurdon's father had been a governor of colonial Connecticut and a famous cleric. Both men are mentioned in Joshua Hempstead's diary of New London, and I had learned about them there. But I didn't connect the family to what still seems to me like the very heart of enslavement, the buying of human beings in Africa.

My error came from not understanding the context in which New England was both a holder of slaves and an agent of making slaves. Without realizing it, I had given New England the largely passive role that many of its own self-histories promulgated. I had suggested that the author of the logbooks was the son of an obscure farmer, never thinking that the likeliest candidate for the log keeper might be a local aristocrat, the descendant of governors on both his mother's and his father's sides, as well as a descendant of the John Winthrop who led Puritans to the New World in 1630 and said, "For we must consider that we shall be as a city upon a hill. The eyes of all people are upon us."

I had looked at slavery but not at the harsh world in which it was part of everyday life. Both John Easton and Dudley Saltonstall operated at various times as privateers, Saltonstall with notable success. Sailing aboard privately owned ships, they held permission from the government to harass enemy ships and take their goods and money. That permission was called a *letter of marque.* The *Africa,* the ship that opens this story, was later confiscated by an English court of law after

it was captured while allegedly trading with the French on the island of Monte Christi at a time when that trade was illegal. (Gurdon
Saltonstall vigorously insisted that Monte Christi was a free neutral
port and denied the charges, but the *Africa* was taken into the harbor
of Port Royal and claimed as a prize by the British. In another lawsuit
stemming from that unlucky voyage, a New London mariner named
Thomas Bolles sued Gurdon for back wages up to the point when the
ship was seized, though Gurdon's defense probably was that the sei-
zure of the vessel terminated his liability for those wages.) A ship's
captain or a vessel could function in several capacities, some of them
perfectly legal, others less so.

In the middle of the eighteenth century, the world of maritime trade
was one of danger, deceit, and death, and it all felt familiar to men like
Easton, and Taylor, and Saltonstall. Their world was driven by profits
from a trade that today we judge to be inhuman, but they would not
have thought the slave trade evil. It was a difficult enterprise, at which
they were skilled and which rewarded them. They were respected in
their communities, and trusted with the property, livelihoods, and
money of others. There is evidence that Saltonstall was a tender father
and a good provider for his family.

The difficulty of making a judgment about the character and nature
of their experience is that even all the details we amass cannot put us
back there, on board the *Africa*, or the *Good Hope*, or the *Fox*. We can
read the accounts of the ghastly smell of slave ships, and know that
other ships avoided them because of that smell, but we cannot be there
on those decks or in those hot and airless compartments. We cannot
fully encompass the suffering.

In their book *Testimony: Crises of Witnessing in Literature, Psychoanalysis and History*, Shoshana Felman and Dori Laub say that massive
trauma "precludes its registration," and that "the observing and recording mechanisms of the human mind are temporarily knocked out,
malfunction." Laub, a psychiatrist and Holocaust survivor, has spent
much of his career examining the effects of trauma, and says that not

knowing is an active process of destruction. Testifying about trauma is essential if we are to attempt to understand, and live with, history that is unbearable.

This book is testimony to a history that I struggle to understand, the history of my homeland allying itself with human enslavement. I thought that if I excavated the details of the ships' logs, and learned about those men and the places they sailed, and knelt on the West African earth where black people were sold, I would *understand* this history. I thought that if I took on this history, and studied its many strands, I would be able to comprehend the empathic failure that allowed it to happen. And the damage that followed—my country's failure to eradicate the racial prejudice that has lived on after slavery —that, too, I would be able to understand.

But history is elusive, and it is easier to find facts in the records of long ago than to understand them. The system of enslavement that prevailed in the Caribbean and the American colonies meets all the modern criteria for a genocidal action, yet books on genocide do not include this history. It is not described that way, or understood as a killing action against black people, even though it killed them as they were being traded, killed them on the ships that ferried them into enslavement, and killed them once they got where they were going.

One night, I read to my mother from a long chapter I was writing for an earlier book of mine. She had lost her glasses—I remember the administrator at the residence saying, "It's time to check some other old faces"—but I looked up from the page to see her leaning forward, looking at me as if she needed to say something urgently, as if I had reminded her of something.

"You know, *my* daughter is writing a book," she said, as if to suggest that I might know her daughter.

I helped her into bed, doing the small rituals she had once done for me. Did she need some water? Was she warm enough? Did she want to keep her socks on? She seemed so small in my arms, and made soft mewing sounds as I smoothed balm on her lips.

What stays with you latest and
deepest? of curious panics,
Of hard-fought engagements or
sieges tremendous what deepest remains?

WALT WHITMAN

An estimated 367,000 captives were brought into the American colonies, but by 1860 there were 4 million held in slavery. The American Colonization Society's plan for sending free black people back to Africa hadn't worked; the cost of the kind of emancipation program Great Britain had enacted in the Caribbean was prohibitive; and as even Abraham Lincoln remarked during a stump visit to New Haven in 1860, no one could agree on a way to end slavery.

Even as the South explored ways to expand slavery and reopen the international slave trade, the North was revising its own earlier role with enslavement, while still milling tons of slave-grown cotton, and producing cotton gins, plantation hoes, and carriages for rich planters. The process of forgetting a once-active relationship with slavery picked up speed as the wealth of those early trading generations underwrote commerce and prosperity for a new century.

A relationship that had once been out in the open was gradually submerged until it could not be seen at all. A man who had watched African children dying of the flux became a commissioned naval officer and successful privateer. In his probate inventory, Dudley Saltonstall had a "Mansion & Garden" in New London and lands to bequeath. His wife, Frances, had died in 1787, so his worldly goods and properties appear to have gone to his children—his guns and shoe buckles, books, Bibles, and globes. He left his "picture of Dr. Franklin" to his son Dudley, who had been educated at Yale and at Tapping Reeve's law school in Litchfield. When Dudley Saltonstall died of a fever in the West

Indies in 1796, he was still a merchant and a mariner, and if the surviving dates are right, he was about fifty-eight. The first federal census, made in 1790, showed that he owned one slave. From an ancient cemetery above the Thames River in New London, I imagined Dudley Saltonstall aboard the *Africa* on that January day in 1757, getting squared away in the tiny space that would have been his, and preparing to make his first notations on wind direction, the ship's course, the hour, and the weather. I wonder if he imagined, on that bitterly cold first day, the world into which he was about to sail, though his father was already part of it as a ship owner and trader. New London was always home base, the place to which Dudley returned. His father and grandfather are buried here on this hillside under a table stone bearing a carving of the Saltonstall family crest: a dragon-like bird rising from a king's coronet. The names on many of the other stones—Coit and Christopher, Mumford and Shaw—would also have been familiar to him, and he would have known their ships and the voyages they made.

By keeping the ships' logs, he left a history, and a story that can be explored but never fully understood. Saltonstall wrote a piece of America's story, one that will never dovetail with the way we want to feel about our country. This piece of the story never did fit, but it never went away either. The story of a marginalized people also was placed in the margins. Their tragedies and uncertainties, their suffering, and the killing realities of their lives were removed from the shared larger narrative and made a chapter, merely.

And yet, slavery was never just a chapter. It was a world that, if we could go back, we would see turned every wheel and brought prosperity into our grasp. We would recognize it as our own. Those people who were described as property, as people with only one name, we would see them—and not as living at the edges of our new world, but as central to it, as its very sinew.

At the farthest edge of the ancient burial ground, down the slope from the Saltonstalls' large stone, there is a group of very small stones, as old as many of the others yet set apart. These men and women were the slaves of New London families. One of the graves is that of Florah, who belonged to Captain Titus Hurlbut, a soldier and trader. She was forty-four when she died in 1764. Twenty-two years earlier, Joshua Hempstead had noted in his diary that there had been a "sad accident" at Captain Hurlbut's home, when a kettle of boiling liquid broke the rod on which it was suspended over the fire and splashed onto a Negro man named Caesar and the infant he held in his lap. The burned child died the next day, while Caesar and another of his children were severely scalded on their legs. I could not find evidence that Caesar and Florah were married, though Florah was, in 1742, the right age to have been mother of an infant and young children; and it was not unusual, in New London at that time, for a black family to be owned by a white family. In 1765, the year after Florah's death, a church record shows that "Titus Hurlbut's Caesar" married a woman named Rebecca, and both are identified as Negroes. Of the headstones near Florah's, none bears the name of Caesar.

On Florah's headstone, the traditional winged angel's head has weathered to resemble a springy-haired African mask with a fierce and terrible gaze. She faces away from the river that may have brought her here. A flat, modern piece of cast metal has been imbedded in the earth in front of the headstone, and it bears the information about Florah's life and death. On the deeply eroded headstone, all the carved words have fallen away, and nothing remains but a woman's face.

...e Imployd abo rigging Carp. & Joiner making awning
...r Making a Pump Can   No Trade at all

...rday July 15th 1758 this 24 hours Light Winds & pleast. Wea.
... Imployd overhawling Blocks Carp. & Joiner Making
...g   No Trade only Bought Some Corn & plantins

...y July 16th   this 24 hours Light Winds & pleast. Weat. People
...yd abo. Jobs Carp. & Joiner abo. the awning the Cap. or
Wanton   Purchased one boy Slave of Quaquome

...day July 17. this 24 hours Light Winds & pleast. Wea. Geop
...yd over hawling tobacco Carp. & Joiner abo. the awning
...de at all   Saild for Surrenam the Large Dutch Sh
...500 & od Slaves onboard

...ay July 18. this 24 hours Light Winds & pleast. Wea. People
...y in ye Hold & fetching Brazeal Tobacco from a Dutch
Cap. Buley   Purchased one man Slave

...sday July 19. this 24 hours Light Winds but a Large Se
...e Imployd picking Tobacco No Trade at all

...day July 20. this 24 hours Calm & little Wind People Imploy
...Hold Cooper a Cutting Rum Hhd Purchased Two Slave
...sely in ye Rhode Except Three Poor Rum Men
...d the yaul up to Clean   broaght a bl Beef

...y July 21 this 24 hours Calm Weather People Imployd over
...ld & found a Hogs. No 86 Leaked all out No 85 only 54 Gal. in be
...gin to ye Cap.   Leakage ocationd by all ye Head Hoops fly
...ade this 24 hours   the agred with my Lord to Send a man
to accraw after ye Longboat for 4 Gal. Trade Rum

...rday July 22. this 24 hours Calm Wea. People Imployd fill
...ready with Water & with Rum Cooper a Cutting Hogs
...d from ye Longboat by a Letter from Underwood w
...at Mumford with 3 Slaves on board

...day July 23. this 24 hours Calm & hazey Weather at 10
...ye Ship to W. Ward which we Suppos'd to be the English Man of

Afterword

My father was a civil rights lawyer. He died before I found the log-books of a Connecticut slave trader and followed them to Africa, and though I wish I could have talked to Dad about the history I am helping to recover, maybe that isn't necessary. Maybe it is enough that I know what *he* did, and that what I'm doing now is the work he showed me. In Sierra Leone, West Africa, I learned a cherished proverb: *That the path not die.*

My father was one of a group of lawyers who began, in the 1950s, to work to integrate the federal service, and to study the reasons there were not more black men and women working in federal jobs.

Born into a Boston family that was poor, my father did not go to college. He attended law school at night, and was nearly thirty before passing the Massachusetts bar. He had graduated from high school in 1931, and worked as a laborer for nearly a decade.

He understood, in the most direct way, that good work—the kind of steady, remunerative work where the individual is treated with dignity—could lift a person from poverty. He joined the federal service because he wanted to have a steady paycheck, but by then his harsh early life had showed him what it was to be poor and invisible.

During most of my girlhood, Dad traveled around New England, visiting post offices, veterans' hospitals, shipyards, and government offices to study the entrance exams and test scores of black job applicants and to ask questions. He was looking for patterns of racial discrimination in hiring, and he found them. He saw that hard work was not enough to create a place for black men and women in the white-collar world of federal service. He was a person of great severity, and he used his own aspirations for a better life to help create jobs for them.

Much later, I understood that his work was a source of grief to him, because progress was slow and change so hard to effect. He went to hear Martin Luther King Jr. speak in the early 1960s and, when he came home, repeated to me what Dr. King had said about the black man waiting at the door for an opportunity. "The black man is knocking at the door. Will you let him in?" Dad repeated, then began to sob terribly, and put his head in his hands. I had never seen my stern, dignified father weep, and I was frightened, but felt that I could not leave him alone at the table as he wept.

People who suffer in early life are hard to surprise, so perhaps Dad wouldn't have been surprised that in personal sorrow and a sorrowful history, I found my way to this book that holds two stories: a history of three Connecticut logbooks, and my mother's decline and death from dementia.

At the same time that I explored the story contained in the logbooks of a New London slave ship officer, I also helped to care for my beautiful mother and shared the stony path of her descent. Her profound memory loss and the damage it caused her led me to question how historical memory is made, and then lost. We say that we cannot change the past, but what happens if we don't *know* the past? How successfully can we manage and fully inhabit the present? I believe that our nation's submerged and incomplete memory of enslavement can be reclaimed, and that if we reclaim and own this history, the future holds the possibility of justice and parity for African Americans. The founders' dream of a democratic society could finally and fully include the black people it excluded.

Dad was a complicated person, but his thinking about racial equality was straightforward. He thought that black men and women should have the same chances he had had, and that if they had equal access to good jobs, their place within American society and culture would become indistinguishable from that of white people. Good work would mean freedom.

To the story of two Connecticut slave ships, and to the story of my mother, I have tried to serve as a witness. Each helped me to understand the other. Both are about the power and importance of memory and the catastrophe of its loss. Both are about a past that has, for me, not ended.

Acknowledgments

For the first book I helped write, I interviewed many scholars, but the process of this book has been different. I already had the soul for this second book, so I read deeply in the work of numerous scholars who I thought would be able to keep me on the right track or who were recommended to me. Many of their names are in the bibliography.

I am very grateful to Suzanna Tamminen and Leslie Starr of Wesleyan University Press, because they made me welcome and supported this work so wholeheartedly. They heard me, and cherished me, and treated me like a friend.

My friends have all been generously and endlessly willing to talk about this work, and gave me many opportunities to think aloud with them. I am grateful always, to Gail Christie and Mark Stephens; Everett and Diane Clowes and Mr. Owl; Marjorie W. DeBold and her late husband Richard DeBold, PhD; Robert P. Forbes, PhD; Jenifer Frank; Angela Keiser; Gayle Kranz and George Greider; Lisa Johnson; Anne D. LeClaire; Joanne Nesti; Brenda Miller; Kimberly Sheridan; Patricia and Clay Sutton; Shirley Wajda, PhD; and Iris Van Rynbach. To Lyn May, for our wonderful long lunches at Pub d'Ivoire and breakfasts at Jack's Country Restaurant, I am profoundly grateful. Joseph Opala opened the world of Bence Island to me and accompanied me to Sierra Leone, West Africa, and I will be in his debt, always.

When I say I cannot thank Douglas Conroy enough, it is only the truth. An attorney who turned to scholarship during retirement, Doug is a student of the illegal trade between the Connecticut colonies and the French during the Seven Years' War. As an English colony, Connecticut was prohibited from trading with England's enemy, France, but of course, the colonists didn't let that stop them, and some of the slave ship captains who were part of my research were also part of that illegal ebb and flow during the eighteenth century. Doug shared hundreds of pages of early documents with me, and copied materials that he thought would prove helpful and have. He was key to the identification of Dudley Saltonstall as the most probable keeper of the logs, and in giving me a real person to research, Doug shaped the book more than I can say.

Robert S. Capers, PhD, was greatly helpful in obtaining many rare eighteenth-century texts, while Deborah Shapiro, executive director of the Middlesex County Historical Society, wisely steered me toward account books and other documents in her society's collections. Executive director Edward Baker and librarian Tricia Royston at the New London County Historical Society could not have been more helpful and encouraging, and I recall happy hours poring over the society's Saltonstall Papers while Edward wrote about the War of 1812 and Tricia researched wiggy questions from the public. To scholar and journalist Stephen D. Courtney I also owe a great debt, because in 2004, he sent me the news article about the logbooks and thus sent me on the path to Sierra Leone and Bence Island. Executive director Kendall F. Wiggin and his staff at the Connecticut State Library, where the logbooks live, were thoroughly helpful and supportive of this project, and made my many hours there a joy. Late in the process of verifying footnotes, Diana McCain and Sierra Dixon at the Connecticut Historical Society were cheering and helpful.

I am deeply in the debt of Jack Davis, Brian Toolan, Clifford Teutsch, and G. Claude Albert, the news executives at the *Hartford Courant* who supported this work and who believed in it.

To Tom Brown, whose photographs of Sierra Leone and Bence Island appear in this book, I am wholly grateful for his generosity and vision. From the moment he learned of this book project, he was on board and helping in every way. With videographer Alan Chaniewski, we shared the experience of being in West Africa in 2004, and left part of ourselves there. Alan's warm, steady presence and calm approach helped keep us on an even keel during often trying circumstances. Not many men can keep their cool while being robbed at gunpoint.

My brother, Charles Farrow, and my sister, Kate Stoddard, lived this story with me, and their love and interest never wavered. Together, we cared for our dear parents unto death, and our bonds can never be broken.

And always, always, in all ways, I am grateful to my dear husband, Stephen Wittman Taylor. He supported me, joyfully and generously, during the writing of this book, and gave me courage. "This is your *work*," he would say. I dedicate this book to him because I could not have written it without him.

Notes

[ONE] RECOVERING THE STORY

Page 1: *Fair & clear & very Cold,* Joshua Hempstead, *The Diary of Joshua Hempstead, 1711–1758,* p. 680.

Page 1: *The wind from the northwest, Log Book of Slave Traders between New London, Conn., and Africa* (hereafter *The Logbooks*), p. 1.

Page 1: *Fair-haired and stocky,* Louis Arthur Norton, *Captains Contentious: The Dysfunctional Sons of the Brine,* "The Naval Patrician," p. 64.

Page 2: *Inside the front cover, The Logbooks,* p. 1. Also see Dava Sobel and William Andrewes, *The Illustrated Longitude: The True Story of a Lone Genius Who Solved the Greatest Scientific Problem of his Time,* "Imaginary Lines," pp. 1–13.

Page 4: *We are who we are,* Eric Kandel, *In Search of Memory: The Emergence of a New Science of Mind,* p. 10.

Page 4: *Mulatto Jack arrived,* Arna Alexander Bontemps, *The Punished Self: Surviving Slavery in the Colonial South,* p. 25.

Page 4: *Colo. Bassetts Abram,* Bontemps, *The Punished Self,* p. 25.

Page 4: *A fierce lightning storm,* Bontemps, *The Punished Self,* p. 31.

Page 4: *But judged by the way,* Bontemps, *The Punished Self,* p. 47.

Page 5: *Adam mowed,* Hempstead, *The Diary,* p. 354.

Page 5: *Adm Carted,* Hempstead, *The Diary,* p. 468.

Page 7: *The men ate, The Logbooks,* p. 85.

Page 7: *A seaman named Denis Bryan, The Logbooks,* p. 38.

Page 7: *A savageness of spirit,* Marcus Rediker, *The Slaveship: A Human History,* p. 220.

Page 10: *The* Africa *weathered, The Logbooks,* pp. 3, 4, 5.

Page 10: *The heavy longboat, The Logbooks,* p. 7.

Page 10: *A seaman named Waterman, The Logbooks,* p. 7.

Page 10: *He sent ashore, The Logbooks,* p. 30.

Page 10: *Captain Easton went ashore, The Logbooks,* p. 30.

Page 10: *An Irish trader,* Nicholas Owen, *Journal of a Slave-Dealer: A View of the Remarkable Axcedents,* p. 68.

Page 10: *Of the estimated 12.5 million,* David Eltis and David Richardson, *Atlas of the Transatlantic Slave Trade,* p. xvii.

Page 12: *From the Sierra Leone region,* Eltis and Richardson, *Atlas of the Transatlantic Slave Trade,* pp. 18–19.

Page 12: *The accepted estimate,* Joseph E. Inikori and Stanley L. Engerman, "From Guesses to Calculations," in Philip Curtin, *The Atlantic Slave Trade: Problems in World History,* p. 37.

Page 13: *Easton also pursued, The Logbooks,* pp. 34, 35.

Page 13: *No sooner had [the chief mate] left me,* William Smith, *A New Voyage to Guinea,* p. 18.

Page 13: *Under Sail bound for Serrelone, The Logbooks,* p. 36.

Page 13: *When Englishman John Hawkins,* Susan Ronald, *The Pirate Queen: Queen Elizabeth I, Her Pirate Adventurers, and the Dawn of Empire,* p. 71.

Page 15: *The next Morning,* John Atkins, *A Voyage to Guinea, Brasil and the West-Indies,* p. 39.

Page 15: *Easton and Saltonstall anchored, The Logbooks,* p. 38.

Page 16: *[We] catcht him, The Logbooks,* p. 38.

Page 16: *For the next week, The Logbooks,* p. 38.

Page 16: *Mentions having a fitt, The Logbooks,* p. 38.

Page 16: *Great Britain's home office,* William St. Clair, *The Door of No Return: The History of Cape Coast Castle and the Atlantic Slave Trade,* pp. 1–2.

Page 16: *The information that survives,* Jay Coughtry, *The Notorious Triangle: Rhode Island and the African Slave Trade, 1700–1807,* p. 249. See the Trans-Atlantic Slave Trade Database, voyage 36218, www .slavevoyages.org.

Page 17: *Sorriest episodes in American naval history,* Norton, *Captains Contentious,* p. 83.

[TWO] THE HAUNTED LAND

Page 21: *A friend sent me,* "Connecticut Slavers Plied African Trade: New London Craft in Eighteenth Century Scoured West Africa for Human Cargoes," *Hartford Times,* Jan. 3, 1928, p. 25.

Page 22: *Not seen because not looked for.* This phrase is my adaptation of a line from T. S. Eliot's poem "Little Gidding" and is to suggest the ways that, in history and in life, we overlook the unexpected. Eliot wrote, "Not known, because not looked for." T. S. Eliot, *The Complete Poems and Plays, 1909–1950*, p. 145.

Page 22: *Their bright ironical names*, Robert Hayden, "Middle Passage."

Page 22: *Roughly one-third died*, Adam Hochschild, *Bury the Chains: Prophets and Rebels in the Fight to Free an Empire's Slaves*, p. 63.

Page 23: *English settlers made an Eden-like Caribbean*, Richard Dunn, *Sugar and Slaves: The Rise of the Planter Class in the English West Indies, 1624–1713*, p. xx.

Page 23: *The heartless sugar system*, Dunn, *Sugar and Slaves*, p. xviii.

Page 23: *It cost less to import a life*, David Brion Davis, *Slavery and Human Progress*, p. 33.

Page 23: *Widow of a North Carolina collector*, *The Logbooks*, Introduction.

Page 26: *His spelling was highly phonetic*, *The Logbooks*, pp. 4, 7, 11.

Page 26: *In the Africa*, *The Logbooks*, pp. 1–2.

Page 27: *On Board the* Good Hope *Lying at Bence Island*, *The Logbooks*, p. 37.

Page 33: *The newspaper ombudsman*, *Hartford Courant*, Feb. 22, 1998, http://articles.courant.com.

Page 35: *And this also has been*, Joseph Conrad, *Heart of Darkness*, p. 19.

Page 36: *In coming in from the sea*, John Matthews, *A Voyage to the River Sierra-Leone on the Coast of Africa*, p. 22.

Page 39: *She called him the old Gentleman*, Anna Maria Falconbridge, *Narrative of Two Voyages to the River Sierra Leone During the Years 1791, 1792*, p. 22.

Pages 42: *On a rocky eminence*, Barry Unsworth, *Sacred Hunger*, p. 307

Page 43: *I suppose it is about one hundred feet in length*, Anna Maria Falconbridge, *Narrative of Two Voyages*, pp. 10–11.

Page 44: *Elegant range of buildings*, Joseph Corry, *Observations Upon the Windward Coast of Africa*, p. 3.

Page 45: *This Day I Dind and Suped*, *The Logbooks*, p. 38.

Page 45: *This is probably the same John Stephens*, Richard Hancock, *Citizens of the World: London Merchants and the Integration of the British Atlantic Community, 1735–1785*, p. 220.

Page 45: *The White Man's Grave*, Philip Curtin, "'The White Man's Grave': Image and Reality, 1789–1850," pp. 94–110.

Page 45: *Drinking away their senses*, Hochschild, *Bury the Chains*, p. 25.

Page 45: *The sacrifices to Bacchus commenced*, Joseph Hawkins, *A Voyage to the Coast of Africa, and Travels into the Interior of That Country*, p. 15.

Page 46: *He witnessed the very dejected*, Atkins, *A Voyage to Guinea*, p. 41.

Page 46: *He seemed to disdain*, Atkins, *A Voyage to Guinea*, pp. 41–42.

Page 46: *If approved, you then agree upon*, Christopher Fyfe, *A Sierra Leone Inheritance*, p. 72.

Page 48: *Involuntarily I strolled to one of the windows*, Anna Maria Falconbridge, *Narrative of Two Voyages*, pp. 23–24.

Page 49: *Delph platter and chocolate bowles*, John Easton, *Wills and Codicils, Inventories*.

Page 49: *Collected landscapes and paintings*, Hancock, *Citizens of the World*, pp. 444–45.

Page 49: *Women and children comprised*, Judith Carney, *Black Rice: The African Origins of Rice Cultivation in the Americas*, p. 71.

Page 50: *I am inclined to think*, James Stanfield, *Observations on a Guinea Voyage, in a Series of Letters Addressed to the Rev. Thomas Clarkson*, p. 19.

Page 51: *Interruption of kinship systems*, Patrick Manning, *Slavery and African Life: Occidental, Oriental, and African Slave Trades*, p. 2.

Page 51: *To remove Negroes then*, Atkins, *A Voyage to Guinea*, p. 178.

Page 52: *The captives could not imagine*, Rosalind Shaw, *Memories of the Slave Trade: Ritual and the Historical Imagination in Sierra Leone*. Chapter 2, "Spirit Memoryscape," pp. 46–69, is particularly helpful. Tufts University anthropology professor Rosalind Shaw studied the memory of the slave trade among Temne people in Sierra Leone and found that although it is not often discussed, the damage from the trade can be seen in the spiritual lives and practices of the Temne, and in the ways that once-benevolent spirit guides became malevolent beings who stole people from their villages. There are, she points out, many ways to remember.

Page 53: *Sugar, sugar, eh? All* that *sugar!*, Peter Fryer, *Staying Power: The History of Black People in Britain*, p. 19.

Page 56: *Transform tidal swamps*, Carney, *Black Rice*, p. 91.

Page 57: *Would deserve the approbation*, Corry, *Observations Upon the Windward Coast*, p. 5.

Page 57: *In many other instances*, Corry, *Observations Upon the Windward Coast*, p. 5.

Page 57: *Quite clean and neat,* Anna Maria Falconbridge, *Narrative of Two Voyages,* p. 20.

Page 57: *Her feeling for him,* Anna Maria Falconbridge, *Narrative of Two Voyages,* p. 95.

Page 58: *A very pretty exercise,* Fyfe, *A Sierra Leone Inheritance* p. 71.

Page 58: *Captain Cleavland sailed past, The Logbooks,* p. 35.

Page 58: *Anna Maria Falconbridge saw,* Anna Maria Falconbridge, *Narrative of Two Voyages,* p. 20.

Page 59: *Through the influence of his own son,* Henry Laurens, *A Letter from Henry Laurens to His Son John Laurens, August 14, 1776,* p. 9.

Page 60: *Some wet blowing weather,* Alexander Falconbridge, *An Account of the Slave Trade on the Coast of Africa,* pp. 24–25.

Page 60: *The Edless, The Logbooks,* p. 34.

Page 60: *Some of the slaves were not very well, The Logbooks,* p. 39.

Page 61: *With 150 Prime Slaves on Board, The Logbooks,* p. 38.

Page 61: *Negroes and Elephants teeth,* William Snelgrave, *A New Account of Some Parts of Guinea and the Slave-Trade,* p. 14.

Page 61: *Which, to the great scandal,* Snelgrave, *A New Account,* p. 14.

Page 64: *One slave for every ton over that,* Susan Schwartz, ed., *Slave Captain: The Career of James Irving in the Liverpool Slave Trade,* p. 17.

Page 64: *A crossroad and marketplace of diseases,* Daniel Mannix and Malcolm Cowley, *Black Cargoes: A History of the Atlantic Slave Trade,* p. 109.

Page 64: *The Dolben Act also sought,* Schwartz, ed., *Slave Captain,* p. 30.

Page 65: *A slave ship was an instrument,* Rediker, *The Slaveship,* p. 309.

Page 65: *The stench below decks,* Alexander Falconbridge, *An Account of the Slave Trade,* p. 25.

Page 65: *Your captains and mates,* Hugh Thomas, *The Slave Trade: The Story of the Atlantic Slave Trade, 1440–1870,* p. 291.

Page 65: *Alas! What a scene of misery,* Fyfe, *A Sierra Leone Inheritance,* p. 76.

Page 65: *Slaves Not Very Well, The Logbooks,* p. 39.

Page 66: *This 24 Hours Died, The Logbooks,* p. 46.

[THREE] TROUBLE IN MIND

Page 69: *Belief and seeing,* from the film *Fog of War: Eleven Lessons from the Life of Robert McNamara,* Sony Pictures Classics, 2003.

Page 73: *The connecting* is *the thinking,* Gerald Myers, *William James: His Life and Thought,* p. 178.

Page 74: *Slavery was not,* David Brion Davis, "The Comparative Approach to American History: Slavery," in Laura Foner and Eugene D. Genovese, eds., *Slavery in the New World: A Reader in Comparative History,* p. 61: "A trade which involved six major nations and lasted for three centuries, which transported 10 to 15 million Africans to the New World, and which became a central part of international rivalry and the struggle for empire, cannot be considered as a mere chapter in the history of North America."

Page 75: *Their lives and labor,* Walter Johnson, "King Cotton's Long Shadow," p. 12.

Page 77: *Embitters every enjoyment,* Theodore Dwight, "In Their Own Words," "Complicity: How Connecticut Chained itself to Slavery," *Hartford Courant, Northeast,* Sept. 22, 2002, p. 56–57. Speech delivered May 8, 1794.

Page 78: *To engage the present generation,* Frances Caulkins, *History of New London Connecticut from the First Survey of the Coast in 1612, to 1860,* pp. 2–3.

Page 78: *Ten negro slaves taken to prison,* Caulkins, *History of New London,* p. 409.

Page 78: *At this period,* Caulkins, *History of New London,* p. 359.

Page 80: *The whole party crossed,* Caulkins, *History of New London,* p. 409.

Page 80: *Eventually, they all returned, The Logbooks,* p. 79.

Page 80: *When Venture and three other men,* Anne Farrow, Joel Lang, and Jenifer Frank, *Complicity: How the North Promoted, Prolonged, and Profited from Slavery,* p. 68; Venture Smith, *A Narrative of the Life and Adventures of Venture, A Native of Africa,* p. 68.

Page 81: *A small black girl named Zeno,* Hempstead, *The Diary,* pp. 562–63; see also di Bonaventura, *For Adam's Sake,* p. 147

Page 82: *With the Freshest Advices Foreign and Domestick, A Modern History of New London County, Connecticut,* vol. 1, Benjamin Tinkham Marshall, ed., New York: Lewis Historical Publishing Company, 1922, p. 117. Available through Google Books.

Page 82: *A kind of hell,* John Stedman, *Narrative of a Five Years' Expedition Against the Revolted Negroes of Surinam,* pp. 54–57. Captain Stedman, who was in Dutch Suriname for five years to help quell a series of uprisings by the enslaved, noted in his narrative that "the clang of the whip" and the screams of the slaves went "from morning till night," p. 90. Though he was not an abolitionist, the horrors he witnessed made him physically ill. Also see Ron Chernow, *Alexander Hamilton*, p. 19.

Page 82: *In a system that made*, Johnson, "King Cotton's Long Shadow," p. 12.

Page 82: *The key dynamic force*, Farrow, Lang, and Frank, *Complicity*, p. 48.

Page 83: *To be sold*, *New-London Summary*, July 17, 1761, p. 3.

Page 84: *A voyage to Carolina*, *Accountbook of Samuel Willis, 1765–1778*, p. 111.

Page 84: *The vessel being under Sail*, *New-London Summary*, July 8, 1763, p. 2.

Page 84: *Two Middletown men traded in human beings*, Elizabeth Warner, *A Pictorial History of Middletown*, p. 22.

Page 85: *The Northerner feels redeemed*, Robert Penn Warren, *The Legacy of the Civil War: Meditations on the Centennial*, pp. 59–60.

Page 86: *If we need to be convinced*, Edward Casey, *Remembering: A Phenomenological Study*, p. xix.

Page 90: *Memories are like stories*, Michael Jackson, "Doing Justice to Life," Harvard Divinity School, Mar. 17, 2010, http://www.hds.harvard.edu /news-events/articles.

Page 91: *She has called this process*, Elizabeth Loftus and Geoffrey Loftus, *Human Memory: The Processing of Information*, pp. 113–14. Available through Google Books.

Page 91: *Padded out with guesses*, Peter Englund, *The Beauty and the Sorrow: An Intimate History of the First World War*, p. 7.

Page 91: *The very keel*, William James, *The Principles of Psychology*, p. 179. Available through Google Books.

Page 92: *We can construct alternative explanations*, William Calvin, *A Brief History of the Mind: From Apes to Intellect and Beyond*, p. xv.

Page 92: *The author of both*, Calvin, *A Brief History of the Mind*, p. 185.

Page 92: *An exaggerated expectation*, Daniel Kahneman, "The Surety of Fools," p. 32.

Page 93: *By the ease with which*, Kahneman, "The Surety of Fools," p. 32.

Page 94: *The fragile power*, Daniel Schacter, *Searching for Memory: The Brain, the Mind, and the Past*, pp. 1–14.

Page 94: *Scholar Eric Williams*, David Northrup, *The Atlantic Slave Trade*, p. 10.

Page 95: *Black Americans are still poorer.* The U.S. Department of Health
and Human Services, Office of Minority Health, maintains comprehensive
statistics on the lives and health of African Americans. For an overview
and links to other studies, please see www.minorityhealth.hhs.gov.
Also, a Feb. 2013 report by the Institutes on Assets and Social Policy at
Brandeis University examined the inequalities in home ownership and
wealth accumulation between white Americans and black Americans:
"The Roots of the Widening Racial Wealth Gap: Explaining the Black-
White Economic Divide."

Page 96: *Suffering beyond quantification,* Michael Roth and Charles Salas,
eds., *Disturbing Remains: Memory, History, and Crisis in the Twentieth
Century,* pp. 1–13.

Page 96: *In twenty years of reporting,* Jane Kramer, *The Politics of Memory:
Looking for Germany in the New Germany,* p. xxiv.

Page 97: *A general lack of knowledge,* Daniel Goldhagen, *Hitler's Willing
Executioners: Ordinary Germans and the Holocaust,* p. 5.

Page 97: *Rational, sober children,* Goldhagen, *Hitler's Willing Executioners,*
p. 27.

Page 97: *The world's largest slave society,* David Northrup, *The Atlantic
Slave Trade: Problems in World History,* p. xiv.

Page 98: *An old negro man,* Patricia Schaefer, *A Useful Friend: A Companion
to the Joshua Hempstead Diary, 1711–1758,* p. 21.

Page 98: *Jackson, whose ancestors,* Allegra di Bonaventura, *For Adam's Sake:
A Family Saga in Colonial New England,* p. 38.

Page 98: *Would in my native country,* Venture Smith, *A Narrative of the Life,*
p. 21.

Page 99: *Culture is simply incapable,* Kandel, *In Search of Memory,* p. 29.

[FOUR] A HISTORY THAT DOESN'T "FIT"

Page 101: *Each life, put out, lies down within us,* Galway Kinnell, *Strong Is
Your Hold,* p. 42.

Page 101: *Dudley Saltonstall sailed, The Logbooks,* p. 35.

Page 102: *To embrace the first fair Wind,* Gurdon Saltonstall, Sailing
instructions to William Taylor, Mar. 24, 1758, Newport Court of
Common Pleas, Judicial Archives, Supreme Court Judicial Records
Center, Pawtucket, Rhode Island.

Page 102: *If by the providence of God*, Saltonstall, Sailing instructions.

Page 102: *With a crew of eleven men*, Rhode Island Notarial Records, vol. 7 (1758–1769), pp. 61–62, Newport Court of Common Pleas, Judicial Archives, Supreme Court Judicial Records Center, Pawtucket, Rhode Island.

Page 102: *Three canoes came off the shore*, The Logbooks, p. 70.

Page 102: *Capt. Taylor thought it not safe*, The Logbooks, p. 70.

Page 103: *Very Great Villians*, The Logbooks, p. 71.

Page 103: *Abot a gunshot apart*, The Logbooks, p. 74.

Page 104: *One Boy Slave* and *Some Gold*, The Logbooks, p. 78.

Page 104: *A Dutch ship*, The Logbooks, p. 78.

Page 104: *No trade this 24 hours*, The Logbooks, p. 78.

Page 105: *Hogshead number 86*, The Logbooks, p. 78.

Page 107: *Endeavored to make her Escape*, Pennsylvania Journal, Oct. 26, 1758, p.14.

Page 107: *Which made it conjectured*, Pennsylvania Journal, Oct. 26, 1758, p. 14.

Page 107: *Gurdon Saltonstall brought suit*, Douglas C. Conroy, "New London and the Pre-Revolutionary 'Illicit Trade' with the French West Indies," Part I, 1755–1763 (master's thesis, Trinity College, Mar. 31, 2011), note 52, p. 28.

Page 108: *So that [I] might be enabled*, William Taylor's testimony, Rhode Island Notary Public Records, vol. 7 (1758–1762), Supreme Court Judicial Records Center, Pawtucket, Rhode Island, pp. 61–62.

Page 108: *And how could it be otherwise*, St. Clair, *The Door of No Return*, p. 183.

Page 109: *Treated with great Hospitality*, Elizabeth Donnan, *Documents Illustrative of the History of the Slave Trade to America*, vol. 3, p. 184.

Page 110: *Nathaniel Shaw of New London*, Nathaniel and Thomas Shaw Papers, Sterling Memorial Library, Yale University, Ledger no. 36, Reel no. 21, pp. 94–101.

Page 110: *Incidents are very common*, Donnan, *Documents Illustrative of the History*, vol. 4., p. 336.

Page 110: *At a trading post*, Atkins, *A Voyage to Guinea*, p. 80.

Page 110: *Bro't advice of the Death*, Donnan, *Documents Illustrative of the History*, vol. 3, p. 71 (*Boston Gazette and News-Letter*, Sept. 17, 1764).

Pages 110: *That same year*, Lorenzo Greene, "Mutiny on the Slave Ships," p. 349. Also see Donnan, *Documents Illustrative of the History*, vol. 3, p. 71.

Page 111: *Set Fire to a Quantity of Rum*, Providence Gazette, vol. 5, iss. 247, Oct. 1, 1768, p. 3.

Page 111: *Is greatly embarrassed*, New-London Gazette, Dec. 30, 1785, p. 3.

Page 112: *A moving letter*, Captain Jonathan Parsons to Jeremiah Wadsworth, Nov. 2, 1779, no. 973.3, D522, State Archives, Connecticut State Library.

Page 112: *1 million pounds*, Esther Forbes, *Paul Revere and the World He Lived In*, p. 358.

Page 112: *Rude Unhappy Temper*, Samuel Eliot Morison, *John Paul Jones: A Sailor's Biography*, p. 43.

Page 112: *As tho they were*, Morison, *John Paul Jones*, p. 52.

Page 112: *That you might regain*, J. Gardner Bartlett, *Historical Genealogy of the Saltonstall Family in England and America*, p. 232.

Page 112: *Set a fire that destroyed*, Bartlett, *Historical Genealogy*, p. 210.

Page 113: *Rum and melted Irish butter*, Caulkins, *History of New London*, p. 553.

Page 115: *A handkerchief of limes*, William Smith, *A New Voyage*, p. 39.

Page 116: *Stunke bitterly*, *The Logbooks*, p. 31.

Page 116: *For now we see*, 1 Corinithians 13:12.

Page 117: *I John Easton of Middletown*, John Easton, *Wills and Codicils, Inventories*.

Page 118: *Herman Melville's character Ishmael*, Herman Melville, *Moby-Dick, or, The Whale*, pp. 36–37. Available through Google Books.

Page 118: *John Newton's description*, Rediker, *The Slaveship*, pp. 157–86.

Page 120: *By cash rec'd of him*, Account Book of Samuel Willis, pp. 156, 163.

Page 121: *For its brutality*, Hochschild, *Bury the Chains*, p. 65.

Page 121: *The assumption that*, Davis, *Slavery and Human Progress*, p. 33.

Page 122: *Which he was very good at*, Owen, *Journal of a Slave-Dealer*, p. 68.

Page 122: *Owen very likely assisted*, Owen, *Journal of a Slave-Dealer*, p. 69; also see the Trans-Atlantic Slave Trade Database, voyage no. 21906, www.slavevoyages.org.

Page 122: *Granduour*, Owen, *Journal of a Slave-Dealer*, p. 1.

Page 122: *It was common*, Owen, *Journal of a Slave-Dealer*, p. 68.

Page 123: *Good breeding*, Owen, *Journal of a Slave-Dealer*, p. 68.

Page 123: *It has been been seldom known*, Owen, *Journal of a Slave-Dealer*, p. 72.

Page 123: *Not a simple matter*, Owen, *Journal of a Slave-Dealer*, p. 7.

Page 123: *Over the course*, Eltis and Richardson, *Atlas of the Transatlantic Slave Trade*, p. 201; Henrice Altink, "Free Labour? Women and Work in Slave and Post Slave Societies," Economic History Society 20th Annual Workshop, Nov. 14, 2009; Matthew Kachur, *The Slave Trade*, p. 93.

Page 123: *Only one-half of the women*, Hochschild, *Bury the Chains*, p. 67.

Page 124: *Nearly 2 million, Africans in America*, Part 3, "Map: The Growing New Nation," https://www.pbs.org/wgbh/aia/part3/map3.html (accessed Jan. 6, 2014).

Page 124: *A Gentleman greatly beloved*, New-London Summary, Jan. 26, 1759, p. 3.

Page 125: *Short but painful*, New-London Gazette, June 14, 1774, p. 3.

Page 127: *Largest slaveholder in Middletown*, U.S. Census, 1790, "Complicity: How Connecticut Chained Itself to Slavery," *Hartford Courant, Northeast*, Sept. 22, 2003, p. 11.

Page 128: *Buried a slave girl (No. 92)*, John Newton, *The Journal of a Slave Trader, 1750–1754*, p. 75.

Page 129: *Benjamin's angel turns his face*, Walter Benjamin, *Illuminations: Essays and Reflections*, pp. 257–58.

[FIVE] SEPARATIONS

Page 132: *Nothing of the ruins*, Joseph Opala, "Bunce Island: A British Slave Castle in Sierra Leone" (a national traveling exhibition), "M.C.F. Easmon's Research," p. 13. Easmon's notes are held in the collections of the Sierra Leone National Museum, Freetown, Sierra Leone. http://www.kennesaw.edu/bunceisland/#ExhibitText.

Page 141: *Who knows, when the time*, Stanley Kunitz, "Tristia," *Passing Through: The Later Poems, New and Selected*, p. 36.

Page 148: *For we must consider*, John Winthrop, "City Upon a Hill," Digital ID 3918, http://www.digitalhistory.uh.edu.

Page 149: *When that trade was illegal*, Reginald Marsden, *Reports of Cases Determined by the High Court of Admiralty and Upon Appeal Therefrom*, pp. 228 (Appellant Case before the Lord Commissioners of Appeals in Prize Causes, the *Africa*, Gurdon Saltonstall, Master, Apr. 22, 1760); suit of Thomas Bolles v. Gurdon Saltonstall, New London County Court Records, box 116, folder 17, no. 74, State Archives, Connecticut State Library.

Page 149: *Massive trauma precludes*, Shoshana Felman and Dori Laub, *Testimony: Crises of Witnessing in Literature, Psychoanalysis and History*, p. 57.

Page 151: *What stays with you*, Walt Whitman, "The Wound-Dresser," http://www.poetryfoundation.org.

Page 151: *An estimated 367,000 captives*, Eltis and Richardson, *Atlas of the Transatlantic Slave Trade*, p. 18.

Page 151: *Even Abraham Lincoln*, Abraham Lincoln, Speech in New Haven, Mar. 6, 1860, *Collected Works of Abraham Lincoln*, vol. 4, p. 14, Abraham Lincoln Association, http://quod.lib.umich.edu.

Page 151: *Mansion & Garden*, Estate of Dudley Saltonstall, *New London Probate District Inventory, 1796*, no. 4671, p. 3, State Archives, Connecticut State Library.

Page 153: *Sad accident*, Hempstead, *The Diary*, p. 402.

Selected Bibliography

BOOKS

Alie, Joe A. D. *A New History of Sierra Leone.* London: Palgrave MacMillan, 1990.

Alpern, Stanley B. "What Africans Got for their Slaves: A Master List of European Trade Goods." *African Studies Association* 22 (1995): 5–43.

Arendt, Hannah. *Eichmann in Jerusalem: A Report on the Banality of Evil.* New York: Penguin Books, 1994.

Atkins, John. *A Voyage to Guinea, Brasil and the West-Indies; in His Majesty's Ships the Swallow and the Weymouth.* London: Ward & Chandler, 1737.

Baron, Donna Keith, Edward J. Hood, and Holly V. Izard. "They Were Here All Along: The Native American Presence in Lower-Central New England in the Eighteenth and Nineteenth Centuries." *William and Mary Quarterly*, Third Series, 53, no. 3 (July 1996): 561–86.

Bartlett, J. Gardner. *Historical Genealogy of the Saltonstall Family in England and America.* Photostat copy, 1931. Collections of the Connecticut State Library, CS 71, S179, 1920 OS.

Behrendt, Stephen D., David Eltis, and David Richardson. "The Costs of Coercion: African Agency in the Pre-Modern Atlantic World." *Economic History Review*, New Series, 54, no. 3 (Aug. 2001): 454–76.

Benjamin, Walter. *Illuminations: Essays and Reflections.* New York: Schocken Books, 2007.

Bontemps, Arna Alexander. *The Punished Self: Surviving Slavery in The Colonial South.* Ithaca, NY: Cornell University Press, 2001.

Bosman, Willem. *A New and Accurate Description of thoe Coast of Guinea.* Translated from the Dutch and published in London, 1721.

Brantlinger, Patrick. "Victorians and Africans: The Genealogy of the Myth of the Dark Continent." *Critical Inquiry* 12, no. 1 (Autumn 1985): 166–203.

Calvin, William. *A Brief History of the Mind: From Apes to Intellect and Beyond.* New York: Oxford University Press, 2004.

Cantwell, Anne-Marie, and Diana diZerenga Wall. *Unearthing Gotham: The Archaeology of New York City.* New Haven, CT: Yale University Press, 2001.

Carney, Judith A. *Black Rice: The African Origins of Rice Cultivation in the Americas.* Cambridge, MA: Harvard University Press, 2001.

———. "From Hands to Tutors: African Expertise in the South Carolina Rice Economy." *Agricultural History* 67, no. 3 (Summer 1993): 1–30.

———. "Rice Milling, Gender and Slave Labour in Colonial South Carolina." *Past & Present*, no. 153 (Nov. 1996): 108–34.

Casey, Edward S. *Remembering: A Phenomenological Study.* Indianapolis: Indiana University Press, 1987.

Caulkins, Frances M. *History of New London Connecticut from the First Survey of the Coast in 1612 to 1860.* New London, CT: New London County Historical Society, 2007. First published in 1852.

Chabris, Christopher, and Daniel Simons. *The Invisible Gorilla: How Our Intuitions Deceive Us.* New York: Crown Publishing Group, 2010.

Chernow, Ron. *Alexander Hamilton.* New York: Penguin Books, 2005.

Conrad, Joseph. *Heart of Darkness.* New York: Penguin Books, 1989.

Cooper, Barbara M. "Reflections on Slavery, Seclusion and Female Labor in the Maradi Region of Niger in the Nineteenth and Twentieth Centuries." *Journal of African History* 35, no. 1 (1994): 61–78.

Cooper, Frederick. "The Problem of Slavery in African Studies," *Journal of African History* 20, no. 1 (1979): 103–25.

Corry, Joseph. *Observations Upon the Windward Coast of Africa.* London: Frank Cass, 1968. First published in 1807.

Coughtry, Jay. *The Notorious Triangle: Rhode Island and the African Slave Trade, 1700–1807.* Philadelphia: Temple University Press, 1981.

Crummey, Donald. "Family and Property amongst the Amhara Nobility." Special Issue, "The History of the Family in Africa," *Journal of African History* 24, no. 2 (1983): 207–220.

Curtin, Philip D. *The Atlantic Slave Trade: A Census.* Madison: University of Wisconsin Press, 1969.

———. *Migration and Mortality in Africa and the Atlantic World, 1700–1900.* London: Ashgate, 2001.

———. "The White Man's Grave': Image and Reality, 1789–1850," *Journal of British Studies* 1, no. 1 (Nov. 1961): 94–110.

Davidson, Basil. *Black Mother: The Years of the African Slave Trade.* Boston: Little, Brown, 1961.

Davis, David Brion. *Slavery and Human Progress.* New York: Oxford University Press, 1984.

Deutsch, Sarah. "The Elusive Guineaman: Newport Slavers, 1735–1774." *New England Quarterly* 55, no. 2 (June 1982): 229–53.

Di Bonaventura, Allegra. *For Adam's Sake: A Family Saga in Colonial New England.* New York: W. W. Norton, 2013.

Dolin, Eric Jay. *Leviathan: The History of Whaling in America.* New York: W. W. Norton, 2007.

Donnan, Elizabeth. *Documents Illustrative of the History of the Slave Trade to America.* Getzville, NY: William S. Hein, 2002 (reprint edition).

Dresser, Madge. *Slavery Obscured: The Social History of the Slave Trade in an English Provincial Port.* London: Continuum, 2001.

Dunn, Richard S. *Sugar and Slaves: The Rise of the Planter Class in the English West Indies, 1624–1713.* Omohundro Institute of Early American History and Culture, Williamsburg, VA. Chapel Hill: University of North Carolina Press, 1972.

Easton, John. *John Easton, Wills and Codicils, Inventories.* No. 1259, State Archives, Connecticut State Library.

Eliot, T. S. *The Complete Poems and Plays, 1909–1950.* New York: Harcourt Brace Jovanovich, 1980.

Eltis, David, Philip Morgan, and David Richardson. "Agency and Diaspora in Atlantic History: Reassessing the African Contribution to Rice Cultivation in the Americas." *American Historical Review* 112, no. 5 (Dec. 2007): 1329–35.

Eltis, David, and David Richardson. *Atlas of the Transatlantic Slave Trade.* Foreword by David Brion Davis. New Haven, CT: Yale University Press, 2010.

Englund, Peter. *The Beauty and the Sorrow: An Intimate History of the First World War.* New York: Alfred A. Knopf, 2011.

Ericson, David F. *The Debate over Slavery: Antislavery and Proslavery Liberalism in Antebellum America.* New York: New York University Press, 2000.

Fage, J. D. "Slavery and the Slave Trade in the Context of West African History." *Journal of African History* 10, no. 3 (1969): 393–404.

Falconbridge, Alexander. *An Account of the Slave Trade on the Coast of Africa.* New York: AMS Press, 1977. First published in 1788.

Falconbridge, Anna Maria. *Narrative of Two Voyages to the River Sierra Leone during the Years 1791, 1792.* Liverpool, UK: Liverpool University Press, 2000.

Farrow, Anne. "Beyond Complicity: The Forgotten Story of Connecticut Slaveships." *Hartford Courant, Northeast,* Apr. 3, 2005.

Farrow, Anne, Joel Lang, and Jenifer Frank. *Complicity: How the North Promoted, Prolonged, and Profited from Slavery.* New York: Ballantine Books, 2005.

Feinberg, H. M. "New Data of European Mortality in West Africa: The Dutch on the Gold Coast." *Journal of African History* 15, no. 3 (1974): 357–71.

Felman, Shoshana, and Dori Laub. *Testimony: Crises of Witnessing in Literature, Psychoanalysis and History.* New York: Routledge, 1992.

Fitts, Robert. *Inventing New England's Slave Paradise.* Boca Raton, FL: Taylor & Francis, 1998.

Fitzgerald, Frances. "Peculiar Institutions: Brown University Looks at the Slave Traders in Its Past." *New Yorker,* Sept. 12, 2005: 68–77.

Foner, Laura, and Eugene D. Genovese, eds. *Slavery in the New World: A Reader in Comparative History.* Englewood Cliffs, NJ: Prentice-Hall, 1969.

Forbes, Esther. *Paul Revere and the World He Lived In.* Boston: Houghton Mifflin Company, 1942.

Foster, Herbert J. "Partners or Captives in Commerce: The Role of Africans in the Slave Trade." *Journal of Black Studies* 6, no. 4 (June 1976): 421–34.

Fryer, Peter. *Staying Power: The History of Black People in Britain.* London: Pluto Press, 1984.

Fyfe, Christopher. *A Short History of Sierra Leone.* London: Longman, 1962.
———. *Sierra Leone Inheritance.* London: Oxford University Press, 1964.

Goldhagen, Daniel. *Hitler's Willing Executioners: Ordinary Germans and the Holocaust.* New York: Vintage Books, 1997.

Gourevitch, Philip. *We Wish to Inform You That Tomorrow We Will Be Killed with Our Families: Stories from Rwanda.* New York: Picador, 1998.

Greene, Lorenzo J. "Mutiny on the Slave Ships." *Phylon* 5, no. 4 (4th Quarter 1944): 346–54.

Guyer, Jane I. "Household and Community in African Studies." *African Studies Review* 24, no. 2–3 (June–Sept. 1981): 87–137.

Haines, Robin, and Ralph Shlomowitz. "Explaining the Mortality Decline in the Eighteenth-Century British Slave Trade." *Economic History Review,* New Series, 53, no. 2 (May 2000): 262–83.

Hair, P. E. H. "Heretics, Slaves and Witches: As Seen by Guinea Jesuits, 1610." *Journal of Religion in Africa* 28, no. 2 (May 1998): 131–44.

Hair, P. E. H., Adams Jones, and Robin Law, eds. *Barbot on Guinea: The Writings of Jean Barbot on West Africa, 1678–1712*. London: Hakluyt Society, 1992.

Hamilton, Douglas, and Robert J. Blyth, eds. *Representing Slavery, Art, Artefacts and Archives in the Collections of the National Maritime Museum*. London: Ashgate, 2007.

Hancock, David. *Citizens of the World: London Merchants and the Integration of the British Atlantic Community, 1735–1785*. Cambridge: Cambridge University Press, 1997.

Harms, Robert. *The Diligent, A Voyage Through the Worlds of the Slave Trade*. New York: Basic Books, 2002.

Hart, W. A., and Christopher Fyfe. "The Stone Sculptures of the Upper Guinea Coast." *History in Africa* 20 (1993): 71–87.

Hawkins, Joseph. *A Voyage to the Coast of Africa, and Travels into the Interior of That Country; Containing Particular Descriptions of the Climate and the Inhabitants, and interesting particulars concerning the SLAVE TRADE*. Troy, NY: Luther Pratt, 1797.

Hayden, Robert. "Middle Passage." Poetry Foundation, http://www .poetryfoundation.org/poem/171823 (accessed Jan. 6, 2014).

Hempstead, Joshua. *The Diary of Joshua Hempstead, 1711–1758*. New London, CT: New London County Historical Society, 1985. First published in 1901.

Hilton, Anne. "Family and Kinship among the Kongo South of the Zaire River from the Sixteenth to the Nineteenth Centuries." Special Issue, "The History of the Family in Africa," *Journal of African History* 24, no. 2 (1983): 189–206.

Hochschild, Adam. *Bury the Chains: Prophets and Rebels in the Fight to Free an Empire's Slaves*. New York: Houghton Mifflin, 2005.

Hodges, Graham Russell, and Alan Edward Brown, eds. *Pretends to be Free: Runaway Slave Advertisements from Colonial and Revolutionary New York and New Jersey*. New York: Garland, 1994.

Holt, Thomas C. *Children of Fire: A History of African Americans*. New York: Hill & Wang, 2010.

Horton, James Oliver, and Lois E. Horton, eds. *Slavery and Public History: The Tough Stuff of American Memory*. New York: New Press, 2006.

Jackson, Michael. *In Sierra Leone*. Durham, NC: Duke University Press, 2004.

Johnson, Walter. "King Cotton's Long Shadow." *New York Times*, Mar. 30, 2013: 12.

Jones, Adam, and Marion Johnson. "Slaves from the Windward Coast." *Journal of African History* 21, no. 1 (1980): 17–34.

Jordan, Winthrop D. *White Over Black: American Attitudes Toward the Negro, 1550–1812*. Omohundro Institute of Early American History and Culture at Williamsburg, VA. Chapel Hill: University of North Carolina Press, 1968.

Kachur, Matthew. *The Slave Trade*. Slavery in the Americas. New York: Chelsea House, 2006.

Kahneman, Daniel. *Thinking, Fast and Slow*. New York: Farrar, Straus & Giroux, 2011.

———. "The Surety of Fools," *New York Times Sunday Magazine*, Oct. 23, 2011: 30–33, 62.

Kandel, Eric R. *In Search of Memory: The Emergence of a New Science of Mind*. New York: W. W. Norton, 2006.

Karen, Robert. "Shame." *Atlantic Monthly*, Feb. 1992: 40–70.

Kinnell, Galway. *Strong Is Your Hold*. Boston: Houghton Mifflin, 2006.

Kiple, Kenneth. *The Caribbean Slave: A Biological History*. Cambridge: Cambridge University Press, 2002.

Kiple, Kenneth F., and Brian T. Higgins. "Mortality Caused by Dehydration during the Middle Passage." *Social Science History* 13, no. 4 (Winter 1989): 421–37.

Kitching, Gavin. "Proto-Industrialization and Demographic Change: A Thesis and Some Possible African Implications." Special Issue, "The History of the Family in Africa," *Journal of African History* 24, no. 2 (1983): 221–40.

Knox-Shaw, Peter. "Defoe and the Politics of Representing the African Interior." *Modern Language Review* 96, no. 4 (Oct. 2001): 937–51.

Kolchin, Peter. *American Slavery, 1619–1877*. New York: Hill & Wang, 1993.

Kopytoff, Igor. "Slavery." *Annual Review of Anthropology* 11 (1982): 207–30.

Kramer, Jane. *The Politics of Memory: Looking for Germany in the New Germany*. New York: Random House, 1996.

Kunitz, Stanley. *Passing Through: The Later Poems, New and Selected*. New York: W. W. Norton, 1995.

Kup, A. Peter. *A History of Sierra Leone, 1400–1787.* Cambridge: Cambridge University Press, 1962.

Laurens, Henry. *A Letter from Henry Laurens to His Son John Laurens, August 14, 1776.* Introduction by Richard B. Morris. New York: Columbia University Libraries, 1964.

Loftus, Elizabeth, and Geoffrey R. Loftus. *Human Memory: The Processing of Information.* New York: Halsted Press Division of John Wiley, 1976.

Log Book of Slave Traders between New London, Conn., & Africa: The Africa, *John Easton, Commander, Jan. 18–April 10, 1757;* The Good Hope, *Alexander Urqhart, Commander, April 11–May 29, 1757;* The Fox, *William Taylor, Commander, March 28–August 10, 1758.* State Archives, Connecticut State Library.

MacGaffey, Wyatt. "Lineage Structure, Marriage, and the Family amongst the Central Bantu." Special Issue, "The History of the Family in Africa," *Journal of African History* 24, no. 2 (1983): 173–87.

Manning, Patrick. *Slavery and African Life: Occidental, Oriental, and African Slave Trades.* Cambridge: Cambridge University Press, 1990.

Mannix, Daniel P., and Malcolm Cowley. *Black Cargoes: A History of the Atlantic Slave Trade.* New York: Penguin Books, 1977.

Marks, Shula, and Rathbone, Richard. "The History of the Family in Africa: Introduction." Special Issue, "The History of the Family in Africa," *Journal of African History* 24, no. 2 (1983): 145–61.

Marsden, Reginald G. *Reports of Cases Determined by the High Court of Admiralty and Upon Appeal Therefrom, Sir Thomas Salusbury and Sir George Hay, Judges, 1758–1774.* London: William Clowes & Sons, 1885.

Matthews, John. *A Voyage to the River Sierra-Leone on the Coast of Africa.* London: B. White & Son, 1788.

McAdams, Dan P. *The Redemptive Self: Stories Americans Live By.* New York: Oxford University Press, 2006.

Minor, Thomas. *The Diary of Thomas Minor, Stonington, Connecticut, 1653 to 1683.* Lillington, NC: Edwards Brothers, 2001.

Morgan, Kenneth. *Slavery and Servitude in Colonial North America: A Short History.* New York: New York University Press, 2001.

Morison, Samuel Eliot. *John Paul Jones: A Sailor's Biography.* Boston: Little, Brown, 1959.

Mouser, Bruce L. *A Slaving Voyage to Africa and Jamaica, the Log of the Sandown, 1793–1794.* Bloomington: Indiana University Press, 2002.

Mtubani, Victor C. D. "The Black Voice in Eighteenth-Century Britain: African Writers Against Slavery and the Slave Trade." *Phylon* 45, no. 2 (2nd Quarter 1984): 85–97.

Myers, Gerald E. *William James: His Life and Thought.* New Haven, CT: Yale University Press, 1986.

Nathan, Matthew. "Historical Chart of the Gold Coast and the Ashanti." *Journal of the Royal African Society* 4, no. 13 (Oct. 1904): 33–43.

Newton, John. *The Journal of a Slave Trader, 1750–1754.* Edited by Bernard Martin and Mark Spurrell. London: Epworth Press, 1962.

Northrup, David, ed. *The Atlantic Slave Trade: Problems in World History.* Lexington, MA: D. C. Heath, 1994.

Norton, Louis Arthur. *Captains Contentious: The Dysfunctional Sons of the Brine.* Columbia: University of South Carolina Press, 2009.

———. "The Penobscot Expedition: A Tale of Two Indicted Patriots." *Northern Mariner* XVI, no. 4 (Oct. 2006): 1–28.

Ntloedibe, France. "A Question of Origins: The Social and Cultural Roots of African American Cultures." *Journal of African American History* 91, no. 4 (Autumn 2006): 401–12.

Owen, Nicholas. *Journal of a Slave-Dealer: A View of the Remarkable Axcedents in the Life of Nics. Owen on the Coast of Africa and America from the Year 1746 to the Year 1757.* Edited by Eveline Martin. London: George Routledge & Sons, 1930.

Phiri, Kings M. "Some Changes in the Matrilineal Family System among the Chewa of Malawi since the Nineteenth Century." Special Issue, "The History of the Family in Africa," *Journal of African History* 24, no. 2 (1983): 257–74.

Piersen, William D. *Black Yankees: The Development of an Afro-American Subculture in 18th Century New England.* Amherst: University of Massachusetts Press, 1988.

———. "White Cannibals, Black Martyrs: Fear, Depression, and Religious Faith as Causes of Suicide Among New Slaves." *Journal of Negro History* 62, no. 2 (Apr. 1977): 147–59.

Platt, Virginia Bever. "'And Don't Forget the Guinea Voyage': The Slave Trade of Aaron Lopez of Newport." *William and Mary Quarterly,* Third Series, 32, no. 4 (Oct. 1975): 601–18.

Porter, R. "The Crispe Family and the African Trade in the Seventeenth Century." *Journal of African History* 9, no. 1 (1968): 57–77.

Price, Richard, and Sally Price, eds. *Stedman's Surinam: Life in an Eighteenth-Century Slave Society.* Baltimore: Johns Hopkins University Press, 1992.

Rediker, Marcus. *The Slaveship: A Human History.* New York: Viking, 2007.

Richardson, Davis. "Slave Exports from West and West-Central Africa, 1700–1810: New Estimates of Volume and Distribution." *Journal of African History* 30, no. 1 (1989): 1–22.

Ronald, Susan. *The Pirate Queen: Queen Elizabeth I, Her Pirate Adventurers, and the Dawn of Empire.* New York: Harper Perennial, 2007.

Roth, Michael S, and Charles G. Salas, eds. *Disturbing Remains: Memory, History, and Crisis in the Twentieth Century.* Los Angeles: Getty Research Institute, 2001.

Ruggles, Steve. "The Origin of African-American Family Structure." *American Sociological Review* 59, no. 1 (Feb. 1994): 136–51.

Schacter, Daniel L. *Searching for Memory: The Brain, the Mind, and the Past.* New York: Basic Books, 1996.

———. *The Seven Sins of Memory: How the Mind Forgets and Remembers.* Boston: Houghton Mifflin, 2001.

Schaefer, Patricia M. *A Useful Friend: A Companion to the Joshua Hempstead Diary, 1711–1758.* New London, CT: New London County Historical Society, 2008.

Schwartz, Susan, ed. *Slave Captain: The Career of James Irving in the Liverpool Slave Trade.* Liverpool, UK: Liverpool University Press, 2008.

Shaw, Rosalind. *Memories of the Slave Trade: Ritual and the Historical Imagination in Sierra Leone.* Chicago: University of Chicago Press, 2002.

Sheridan, Richard B. "The Guinea Surgeons on the Middle Passage: The Provision of Medical Services in the British Slave Trade." *International Journal of African Historical Studies* 14, no. 4 (1981): 601–25.

Smallwood, Stephanie. *Saltwater Slavery: A Middle Passage from Africa to American Diaspora.* Cambridge, MA: Harvard University Press, 2007.

Smith, Robert. "The Canoe in West African History." *Journal of West African History* 11, no. 4 (1970): 515–33.

Smith, Venture. *A Narrative of the Life and Adventures of Venture, A Native of Africa, But Resident Above Sixty Years in the United States of America.* New London, CT: New London County Historical Society. Originally published in New London in 1798.

Smith, William. *A New Voyage to Guinea.* London: Frank Cass, 1967. First published in London in 1744.

Snelgrave, William. *A New Account of Some Parts of Guinea and the Slave-Trade.* London: James, John & Paul Knatton, 1734.

Sobel, Dava, and William J. H. Andrewes. *The Illustrated Longitude: The True Story of a Lone Genius who Solved the Greatest Scientific Problem of his Time.* New York: Walker, 1995.

Spear, Norman E., and David C. Riccio. *Memory: Phenomena and Principles.* Boston: Allyn & Bacon, 1994.

Stanfield, James F. *Observations on a Guinea Voyage, in a Series of Letters Addressed to the Rev. Thomas Clarkson.* London: James Phillips, George-Yard, Lombard-Street, 1788.

Stauffer, John. *The Black Hearts of Men: Radical Abolitionists and the Transformation of Race.* Cambridge, MA: Harvard University Press, 2002.

St. Clair, William. *The Door of No Return: The History of Cape Coast Castle and the Atlantic Slave Trade.* New York: Blue Bridge, 2007.

Steckel, Richard H., and Richard A. Jensen. "New Evidence on the Causes of Slave and Crew Mortality in the Atlantic Slave Trade." *Journal of Economic History* 46, no. 1 (Mar. 1986): 57–77.

Stedman, John G., *Narrative of a Five Years' Expedition Against the Revolted Negroes of Surinam.* London: J. Johnson, St. Paul's Church, & J. Edwards, Pall Mall, 1796.

Tattersfield, Nigel. *The Forgotten Trade: Comprising the Log of the Daniel and Henry of 1700 and Accounts of the Slave Trade from the Minor Ports of England, 1698–1725.* London: Jonathan Cape, 1991.

Thomas, Dalby. *An Historical Account of the Rise and Growth of the West-India Colonies.* London: Joseph Hindmarsh, 1690. Reprinted in facsimile edition, Arno Press, 1972.

Thomas, Hugh. *The Slave Trade: The Story of the Atlantic Slave Trade, 1440–1870.* New York: Simon & Schuster, 1997.

Thornton, John. "Cannibals, Witches and Slave Traders in the Atlantic World." *William and Mary Quarterly,* Third Series, 60, no. 2 (Apr. 2003): 273–94.

Unsworth, Barry. *Sacred Hunger.* New York: W. W. Norton, 2002.

Vaughan, Megan. "Which Family?: Problems in the Reconstruction of the History of the Family as an Economic and Cultural Unit." Special Issue, "The History of the Family in Africa," *Journal of African History* 24, no. 2 (1983): 275–83.

Warner, Elizabeth A. *A Pictorial History of Middletown.* Greater Middletown Preservation Trust. Norfolk, VA: Donning, 2001.

Warren, Robert Penn. *The Legacy of the Civil War: Meditations on the Centennial.* New York: Random House, 1961.

Warren, Wendy Anne. "The Cause of Her Grief: The Rape of a Slave in Early New England." *Journal of American History* (Mar. 2007): 1031–49.

Wiencek, Henry. *An Imperfect God: George Washington, His Slaves, and the Creation of America.* New York: Farrar, Straus & Giroux, 2003.

Williams, Eric. "The Golden Age of the Slave System in Britain." *Journal of Negro History* 25, no. 1 (Jan. 1940): 60–106.

Wilson, Harriet E. *Our Nig; or, Sketches from the Life of a Free Black.* New York: Vintage Books, 2002.

Wood, Marcus. *Blind Memory: Visual Representations of Slavery in England and America, 1780–1865.* New York: Routledge, 2000.

Woodward, Christopher. *In Ruins: A Journey Through History, Art, and Literature.* New York: Vintage Books, 2001.

Wylie, Kenneth C. *The Political Kingdoms of the Temne, Temne Government in Sierra Leone, 1825–1910.* New York: Africana, 1977.

ACCOUNT BOOKS

Account Book of Middletown Merchant Samuel Starr. Middlesex County Historical Society Collections, 1987.x.12.

Account Book of Samuel Willis, 1765–1778, Middletown Merchant and Importer. Middlesex County Historical Society Collections, 1920.1.1.

Dudley Saltonstall Papers. New London County Historical Society Collections, MsD.Se22; MsD.T795; MsG.688; MsG/Sa37d; MsH.P253; MsJ; MsJ H196; MsJ.M663.; MsJ.Ne29; MsJ.Sa37.; MsJ.Sa37ab; MsJ. Sa37b.; MsJ.Sa37f.; MsJ.T772.; MsJ.W251.; MsJsa37j; MsO.St27b; MsQ. H593.; MsQ.M663 1781; MsQ.W527.; MsQ.W569z; MsZ.

Reading Guide

These questions have been created to help foster
productive and generative discussions around the broad
subjects addressed in *The Logbooks.* They are designed to help
readers examine their own feelings about race in America
and racial disparity, as well as the content of the book.

1. What is your general impression of slavery in America? Was it widespread? Influential? An economic engine? Other than the slaves themselves, who was involved in slavery and what kind of people were they?

2. Do you understand how the United States became a nation that held slaves? How do you feel about this part of the country's history?

3. Was slavery more important in the South than in the North?

4. Have your relatives—grandparents, aunts and uncles, etc.—ever talked about prejudice they encountered? How did it make you feel? Have you ever felt angered or hurt by things that happened a long time ago, even though they didn't happen directly to you?

5. Have you ever refused to buy something because you knew it was made under inhumane conditions?

6. Are we, as a people today, responsible in any way for the past?

7. We say that we cannot change history, but what if we don't *know* our history . . . what happens when we don't have an accurate grasp of what occurred in the past? Should we revisit it and try to make the story whole? How would that help? Or would it not help at all? Would it just make everything worse?

8. How is our sense of the past altered when the people who lived through it are no longer alive?

9. Do you believe that trauma—either in the past or the present—can be buried?

10. Have you ever imagined living without a memory of who you are? Can

you imagine waking up and not recognizing the room you are in? The partner next to you? What would that be like? What if you lost, forever, the ability to remember the people you loved? Or how to do your job, or what you have been doing for the last few decades? What if you looked in a mirror and did not recognize yourself? What different emotions would you feel?

11. Have you known someone who suffered from Alzheimer's disease or dementia? What did you notice about that person? How did it make you feel?

12. Do you feel, generally, that life is fair or unfair? Are you comfortable with what you believe or do you feel, in some way, helpless? Does it make you angry?

13. Why should we care about the past? It's over, right? Why do genealogists and many others trace their families back over centuries? Why does that personal history matter to an individual? Does this new knowledge of old times bring about change of any kind? What do we mean when we say "the apple doesn't fall far from the tree"?

14. Have you ever noticed that you and your partner, sibling, or best friend sometimes remember the same event very differently? What might that mean? How can one individual's cataclysm be a nonevent to a friend or relative?

15. Have you ever committed an act or made a remark that you later regretted? Did you do anything about it?

16. What changes when you discover your history is different from what you thought it was? Would you want to know the truth? What would be different?

17. Is it possible for good people to do things we might judge to be wrong? Do you think John Easton and Dudley Saltonstall thought they were doing anything wrong? What would they have had to say to themselves to be able to do the work they did? How do you think they viewed black people?

18. How should a society deal with a painful memory?

19. If you are an African American, how do you feel about the history of black Americans? If you are a white person, what do you feel when you think about the history of enslaved people in America and the one hundred and fifty years that have followed since slavery was abolished?

20. Do you see America as a nation divided in any way? Do you feel that

America is a just society and one with equal opportunities for people of all colors? What does a just society look like?

21. Does a conversation about slavery in America seem relevant to you? Does slavery in America seem to you like a history that is over and cannot be changed?

22. Do you have a close friend who is a different color than you? Do issues of race ever enter the relationship?

23. Would you like America to be less racially segregated? If you believe the country should be changed, what do you think should happen to bring about that change?

24. Is there something in us that makes us long to have power over another person? Is enslavement the furthest expression of an inherent human impulse?

25. Have you ever imagined your life being taken from you and subjugated to the will of another person? What would it be like to have your family, your culture, and your history taken from you? How would you endure? What would you try to do or create?

26. Is it possible to show empathy for history?

ABOUT THE AUTHOR

Anne Farrow is coauthor of the bestseller
*Complicity: How the North Promoted, Prolonged, and Profited
from Slavery*. She lives in Haddam, Connecticut.

Garnet Books

ABOUT THE DRIFTLESS CONNECTICUT SERIES

The Driftless Connecticut Series is a publication award program established in 2010 to recognize excellent books with a Connecticut focus or written by a Connecticut author. To be eligible, the book must have a Connecticut topic or setting, or an author must have been born in Connecticut or have been a legal resident of Connecticut for at least three years.

The Driftless Connecticut Series is funded by the
Beatrice Fox Auerbach Foundation Fund
at the Hartford Foundation for Public Giving.
For more information and a complete list
of books in the Driftless Connecticut Series,
please visit us online at
http://www.wesleyan.edu/wespress/driftless.